RURAL WOMEN'S LEADERSHIP IN ATLANTIC CANADA

LOUISE CARBERT

Rural Women's Leadership in Atlantic Canada

First-hand Perspectives on Local Public Life and Participation in Electoral Politics

UNIVERSITY OF TORONTO PRESS
Toronto Buffalo London

© University of Toronto Press Incorporated 2006
Toronto Buffalo London
Printed in Canada

ISBN-13: 978-0-8020-9125-3
ISBN-10: 0-8020-9125-3

Printed on acid-free paper

Library and Archives Canada Cataloguing in Publication

Carbert, Louise I. (Louise Irene), 1960–
  Rural women's leadership in Atlantic Canada : first-hand perspectives on
  local public life and participation in electoral politics / Louise Carbert.

  Includes bibliographical references and index.
  ISBN-13: 978-0-8020-9125-3
  ISBN-10: 0-8020-9125-3

  1. Women politicians – Atlantic Province.   2. Women in politics – Atlantic
  Provinces.   3. Atlantic Provinces – Rural conditions.   I. Title.

  HQ1236.5.C2C367 2006   305.43′3209715   C2006-902712-9

This book has been published with the help of a grant from the Canadian
Federation for the Humanities and Social Sciences, through the Aid to
Scholarly Publications Programme, using funds provided by the Social
Sciences and Humanities Research Council of Canada.

University of Toronto Press acknowledges the financial assistance to its
publishing program of the Canada Council for the Arts and the Ontario
Arts Council.

University of Toronto Press acknowledges the financial support for its
publishing activities of the Government of Canada through the Book
Publishing Industry Development Program (BPIDP).

Contents

Acknowledgments

I want to thank all the women who met with me and spoke their minds with immense honesty, sometimes tinged with bitterness, and always tempered with good humour and cleverness. I owe a great debt to the many people who helped me to arrange the interview meetings in small towns across Atlantic Canada. Brigitte Newmann, Denise Moore, and Stella Lord of the Nova Scotia Advisory Council on the Status of Women deserve special thanks for their help throughout the project.

This research was funded in part by a partnership grant from the Shastri Indo-Canadian Institute and the Canadian International Development Agency. I want to thank Sara Ahmed of the University of Ahmedabad for inviting me to join her in this partnership and for her advice in the design of my project in Atlantic Canada. This work was also funded by a research grant from the Social Sciences and Humanities Research Council of Canada.

Thanks go to student research assistants Lidija Perovic, Lisa Whitehead, Monic Wilner, Terri DeLorenzo, Andrea Olive, and Amanda Slaunwhite. Len Sonmor provided valuable assistance and advice in every step of the project. As always, I am grateful for my intellectual discussions with Naomi Black, Katherine Fierlbeck, and Jennifer Smith. The manuscript was improved by the comments and suggestions of anonymous referees. Finally, I would like to thank my children, Adam and Jasper, for being good sports as they were dragged along on their vacations to far-flung reaches of the continent.

RURAL WOMEN'S LEADERSHIP IN ATLANTIC CANADA

1 Introduction

A Rural Deficit

Leadership has many faces. It encompasses a broad spectrum of activities and behaviours that can be lumped together under the rubric of civic engagement. At the highest levels of responsibility is the visible tip of the iceberg: elected office. This is a good place to start a book on rural women's leadership because it is here that we find a well-established and unambiguous indication that something important is amiss in rural areas when it comes to women's participation in public life. Simply put, far fewer women find their way into elected office in rural areas than in urban settings, no matter which level of government is examined – municipal, provincial, or national. This dearth is not limited to a small number of remote outposts but rather extends to an enormous number of communities constituting almost half of Canada, by population and representation, and even higher proportions in some provinces.

To get a feel for the scale of this contrast, consider a specific example that will be familiar to most readers: the 2004 Canadian national election. Nationwide, 21 per cent of the seats in the House of Commons were won by women. But this number pales in comparison with the proportions in the largest metropolitan centres. Women were elected in 36 per cent of the densely populated urban ridings in and around Toronto,[1] the largest Canadian city, and in 38 per cent of the urban ridings in and around Montreal,[2] the second largest. One might contend that comparison with the national average is unfair because these two cities are located in provinces that elected relatively high proportions of women to Ottawa overall – 25 per cent in Ontario and 27 per cent in Quebec. However, these relatively high provincewide numbers are almost entirely attributable to the particularly high numbers in Toronto and Montreal.[3]

Another, even more telling, sense of the rural-urban distinction in the 2004 election can be estimated quite easily in the case of Ontario, because of the particular structure of federal electoral districts in this, the most populous province. Ontario, unlike other provinces, has several urban centres large enough to support one or more federal districts in a concentrated area. A brief look at the electoral map of Ontario reveals that roughly half of the federal districts are this sort of small urban riding, and the rest are much larger in geographical area, encompassing substantial rural areas. Therefore, a simple rural-urban contrast can be achieved by listing the 106 Ontario federal ridings in order of population density and comparing the top and bottom halves of the list.[4] Looking first at the top (more urban) half, we find that in 2004 women were elected in 38 per cent (20 of 53) of the most densely populated Ontario ridings. In the other (more rural) half, only 13 per cent (7 of 53) of the least densely populated districts in Ontario elected women. According to this estimate, in the 2004 national election an urban Ontario riding was almost three times as likely to be won by a woman as was a rural one.

Is it really half of Ontario that created this contrast? Or is the dearth of women elected confined only to the most sparsely populated, highly rural, areas? Dividing the same 106 districts into four groups instead of two, again according to population density, we find that women were elected in 15 per cent (4 of 27) of the most sparsely populated ridings, in 12 per cent (3 of 26) of the second-most rural group, in 42 per cent (11 of 26) of the second-most urban group, and in 33 per cent (9 of 27) of the most densely populated electoral districts. These numbers exhibit a major jump at the halfway mark, showing us that the dearth of women elected indeed extends throughout the least densely populated half of ridings – roughly everywhere outside the largest cities – representing 5.5 million people, or 48 per cent of Ontario's population. This phenomenon is large scale by any measure.

One might imagine trying to interpret this rural-urban contrast in terms of partisan preferences because (1) it is well known that in 2004 Conservative Party support in Ontario was concentrated in rural areas (i.e., fully 22 of the 24 Ontario seats won by the Conservatives were in the least densely populated half of the ridings) and (2) previous studies have associated support for the Reform/Alliance component of this party in other regions with low rates of women elected (Young 2003, 87–8). This sort of argument would not take away from the rural-urban contrast being highlighted here, because distinct patterns of partisan preferences form an important component of that contrast. In any case, Liberal rural

Ontario ridings were no more likely to be won by women than were those that voted Conservative. Of the twenty-two Conservative rural Ontario seats, four (18 per cent) were won by women. By comparison, the Liberals took twenty-eight seats from among the fifty-three least densely populated Ontario ridings, and only three of these (11 per cent) were won by women.[5] Thus, the Liberals were no more proficient than the Conservatives at getting women elected in rural districts. These numbers suggest that the rural deficit should be recognized as a separate independent electoral pattern that goes beyond the partisan characteristics of the district.

Nor can one blame rural voters' sexism for this dearth. That only three Liberal women won seats in the more rural half of the ridings is not evidence of voter hostility, because that party put up only six female candidates in these fifty-three districts. The success rate of the women candidates was quite in line with their Liberal male counterparts (25 winners out of 47 candidates, or 53 per cent).[6] Looking across all political parties is complicated by the relatively large numbers of female candidates who ran for parties that stood no chance of winning their riding, quite apart from the candidate's gender; a fair comparison would exclude such candidates. Counting only competitive parties in each district, women made up 12 per cent (14 of 114) of the candidates in the more rural half of Ontario districts.[7] Since this candidacy ratio approximately matches the proportion of seats won by women (13 per cent or 7 of 53 seats), there is no evidence of gender bias among rural voters. Hence we can attribute the dearth of rural seats won by women to low candidacy levels and not to voter sexism.

This striking example of a rural deficit in the election of women to political office is not an isolated result. Our back-of-the-envelope estimates from this one election are entirely consistent with results of quantitative studies that have consistently found that far fewer women hold elected office in rural areas than in urban metropolitan centres (see, e.g., Matland and Studlar 1998; Brodie 1977; Moncrief and Thompson 1991). This deficit is present at all three levels of government – and holds independently of partisan effects. It extends to every part of the country and has persisted over several decades. The same result has been found in the United States as well.[8] For example, Lisa Bourke and A.E. Luloff suggested that 'it may well be easier for a woman to be voted into Congress than be elected county commissioner of a non-metropolitan county' (1997, 19). Furthermore, the rural deficit is amplified in Canadian legislatures, due to the practice of drawing electoral boundaries in such a way

Figure 1.1 Proportions of women in Canada's national and provincial legislatures, 1964–2004.

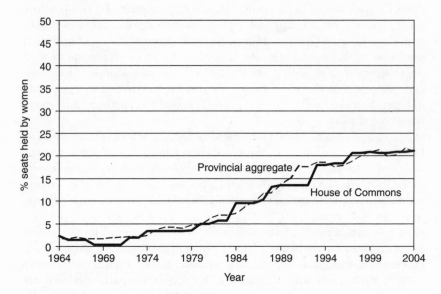

as to create an overrepresentation of rural ridings compared with urban ridings. Matland and Studlar (1998) proposed that this practice helps explain why fewer women are elected to Canadian provincial legislatures than to U.S. state assemblies, where the assignment of electoral districts is based more closely on the principle of 'one person / one vote.' In Canada, a series of court rulings has upheld the principle of effective, not necessarily equal representation, and has thus entrenched the practice of overrepresentation of rural voters. Based on these findings, we can reasonably expect that the political dynamics of rural Canada will continue to exercise a major influence over electoral outcomes for the foreseeable future.

One of those outcomes is that what seemed like progress towards gender parity in Canada's legislatures has stalled. It has become increasingly apparent since the mid-1990s that the long-standing pattern of overall gains in women elected has flagged, at both the federal and provincial levels, with proportions of women plateauing near the 20 per cent mark nationwide. We can see this plateau in both curves of figure 1.1.[9] The two proportions rose nearly in tandem during the period 1964–2004, starting at below 5 per cent throughout the 1960s and 1970s. The rise was most rapid during the 1980s, approaching 15 per cent by the end of that decade. The rate of increase slowed during the 1990s, as the proportions reached 20 per cent near the end of that decade. Both curves reached a plateau thereafter, and the proportion of seats held by women remained near the 20 per cent mark.

Just from looking at the metropolitan estimates discussed above from the 2004 national election, it seems clear that there is only so much potential for further increases in major urban centres. While they are not yet at parity, it would be unrealistic to expect large cities alone to bring up the entire national average by very much in the near future. The more rural districts of Canada would have to play a key role in any significant future overall gains in women's election to public office.

Why should we care that the proportion of women elected to public office has stalled at less than halfway to parity? A good deal of scholarship supports the proposition that the persistence of this stark underrepresentation has important consequences for the future of democracy in Canada. In his quantitative study of electoral democracy in the provinces, Donald Blake highlighted the election of women as standing out in terms of its broad linkage to many cultural, economic, and institutional indicators of electoral democracy (2001, 28). Blake's work contributes solid empirical evidence to earlier theoretical justifications for viewing the election of women as a fundamental component of the quality of electoral democracy. One such argument hearkens back to the nineteenth-century Progressive Era, when women's influence was advocated as a strategy to clean up politics, principally by making it a more sober affair. Contemporary politicians still make a plausible case along these lines. For example, at a workshop drawing together academics and women involved in electoral politics in the Atlantic region, in 2001, member of Parliament (and at that time leader of the New Democratic Party) Alexa McDonough claimed, 'I will say, without hesitation that, in my own experience, women do have a kind of humanising, a politicising, a feminising, civilising effect within political parties' (2003, 141). In a similar vein, former MP Mary Clancy recalled one ordinary supply day when everyone, from the speaker to the pages, was female: 'That was a very peaceful day in the House of Commons' (2003, 79).

In the academic literature, feminist arguments for women's election to public office are usually put in terms of the concepts of substantive representation or the mandate of difference (see, e.g., Phillips 1995; Vickers 1997; Young 1990). Indeed, empirical evidence backs up the expectation that female politicians would represent women's distinct interests by speaking out on salient issues, such as employment equity, reproductive rights, and access to child care. Manon Tremblay's analysis of *Hansard* found that female MPs spoke more frequently and at greater length on women's issues than did male MPs (1998). Similarly, studies of legislative debates at the provincial level have found that female legislators spoke up for women to an extent that their male colleagues did not, especially when they were supported in the legislature by sufficient numbers of other female politicians (Burt and Lorenzin 1997; Trimble 1997).

The mandate-of-difference argument implies that feminist women represent women's substantive interests more effectively than do non-feminist politicians. This distinction is often extrapolated into a general left-right distinction, even to the point of putting feminist men ahead of non-feminist women. For example, Alexa McDonough has consistently and vigorously defended this point of view:

> So, am I in favour of more women? Absolutely yes. Am I in favour of more right-wing women? No. I have to fight to defeat them as much as I can because they give a kind of respectability which is not deserved and which is not going to result in any change. There are women out there who really do care, but it is a false illusion to think that if we have more women from whatever party, everything will get better. I actually think that by far the bigger factor in whether change will occur for women is whether there is a solid progressive left force in the political arena. (2003, 142)

As leader of the New Democratic Party at the time, McDonough could have no other opinion. But where does her advocacy of more left-wing politicians, whether male or female, leave women who do not agree with her on an ideological level?

McDonough's is not the only point of view, even among feminists. Others take the stance that all avenues that bring women to power make a positive contribution, and that women should be elected to represent Canadians all across the ideological spectrum. After all, women are no more homogeneous a group than men are. Linda Trimble and Jane Arscott (2003, 151–2) cited the 'Deb effect' in this regard, which proposes that Deborah Grey, the first Reform Party MP,[10] was an effective politician who made headway for women's leadership, while at the same time maintaining an overall right-wing position.

The most universally persuasive case for parity in women's election to public office rests on democracy. It holds that the representation of women, in all their diversity, confers legitimacy on the entire political system, whether one considers Canada or any other democratic regime.[11] This view is not based on an expectation that women uphold a higher moral standard, a particular ideological perspective, or a more sophisticated level of debate than men do. One does not have to believe that women politicians do a better job than men. Women's increased participation itself contributes to the quality of democracy. By implication, everybody – feminist or not, left-leaning or right-leaning – has a stake in a rise towards gender parity in electoral politics.

Canadian voters seem to be ready for such a rise, as they do not have a problem with voting for a woman. The problem is the small number of women to vote for. For example, in the 2004 general election, women constituted only 22 per cent of the candidates fielded by the four major parties in all 308 districts nationwide. This number matches closely the proportion of seats won by women (21 per cent) implying that voting was approximately gender neutral. Numerous quantitative studies have found this same result in the United States. For example, Darcy, Welch, and Clark examined candidate success rates in state elections and concluded that 'voters were not discriminating against female candidates. There was little difference in voters' reactions to male and female candidates of similar party and incumbency status' (1994, 73). The 2004 Canadian election then conformed to the established continentwide rule that the election of women is not limited by voter hostility but by the small numbers of female candidates running for winnable seats. This is true in both urban and rural settings but the dearth of female candidates is much more extreme in rural areas. The absence of gender bias among voters contrasts sharply with the enormous gender disparity among elected representatives. This juxtaposition turns the issue of women's election away from the vote itself, and towards the recruitment and nomination processes.

An absence is never easy to investigate. Asking why a riding association did *not* choose a woman as its candidate is not really about the closed-door vote that completes the nomination process. In many cases there simply was no woman to vote for at that meeting. Far more to the point is the difficult and open-ended question about the lead-up to the meeting: Who else conceivably could have been chosen instead of the nominated candidate? The pool of *potential* candidates goes beyond those who actually put their names forward. Who is qualified and available but not groomed? Whose qualifications go unrecognized? A good deal of research has addressed the role of party gatekeepers in excluding women as candidates (see Niven 1998, 28–31, 123–5; Trimble and Arscott 2003, 57–64, and citations therein). Far less effort has been directed to the other logical possibility that some women might be excluding themselves: Who is qualified but unwilling to step forward? In either case, the actions of a riding association can be understood meaningfully only if we have a clear idea of whom it had to work with.

Perhaps the greatest challenge in making progress towards understanding why there are so few women candidates is that virtually nothing is known of the pool of potential women candidates. The universal importance of filling this gap in knowledge, and the difficulty of doing so, is a major conclusion of perhaps the most comprehensive and widely cited reference on the topic, that is, Darcy, Welch, and Clark's overview of women and elections throughout the industrialized world. They pointed out that 'trying to figure out who constitutes a pool of potential candidates and then learning the members' reasons for running or not are nearly impossible tasks. So, our conclusions about why women do not run must be based more on inference and less on direct evidence than our conclusions about what happens to women when they do run' (1994, 178).

In Canada, knowledge of the pool of potential women candidates is especially low in rural areas, precisely where rates of women's candidacy and election are lowest and precisely where the task is most daunting logistically. This book presents results from a regional study that confronted this outstanding challenge head-on.

A Hands-On Study in Rural Atlantic Communities

It often makes sense to study a phenomenon where it is most conspicuous. Atlantic Canada[12] has the dual distinction of being more rural than other regions of Canada and of trailing other regions in terms of women holding elected office. We begin here with a brief demonstration of this dual distinction, as context for a regional study that sought out and interviewed rural women leaders who could plausibly comprise a pool of potential candidates for elected office.

Looking again at the 2004 national election, only two of the thirty-two Atlantic seats in the House of Commons were won by women. Both of these were in urban ridings: Claudette Bradshaw in Moncton-Riverview-Dieppe and Alexa McDonough in Halifax. Considering that only seven of the thirty-two Atlantic federal ridings are unambiguously urban,[13] the proportion of urban seats held by women is by no means low, relative to cities elsewhere. In keeping with the established continentwide pattern of gender-neutral voting described above, the shutout in the twenty-five more rural districts followed low women's candidacy levels in winnable ridings. Of the seventy-five candidates running for the three major political parties in these districts, only five were women running in ridings in which their party was at least somewhat competitive; and it is questionable how winnable any of these races could have been considered, as each featured a high-profile male incumbent who ended up winning by a comfortable margin.[14]

With a total of thirty-two Atlantic seats in the House of Commons, calculations of proportions of women elected from Atlantic Canada are quite sensitive to specific events. For example, in the preceding (2000) national election, four of the thirty-two Atlantic seats were won by women, and all four were among the seven urban ridings – that is, beyond parity in the Atlantic cities! The coincidence that both Elsie Wayne (Saint John) and Wendy Lill (Dartmouth) left politics at the same time had the effect of cutting the Atlantic contingent of female MPs by half. None of the twenty-five more rural ridings of Atlantic Canada has elected a woman in the past two national elections. The pattern of women elected to the House of Commons from Atlantic Canada presents a stark rural-urban contrast, but at the same time leaves something to be desired in terms of robustness because federal ridings are so large compared with the population of the region.

The provincial scene gives us a more robust picture of Atlantic Canada because the provincial ridings are much smaller than the federal ridings – all below 25,000 in population. Of the 182 provincial ridings in the four Atlantic provinces, only forty-nine (27 per cent) are confined largely to the six main urban centres: St John's, Charlottetown, Halifax, Saint John, Fredericton, and Moncton. The other 133 ridings (73 per cent) are geographically more extensive and located away from these centres and, thus, can be classified as more rural. Taken together, the many communities in these more rural districts comprise approximately 1.7 million people, representing a dominent force in the Atlantic region and a not insignificant component of the national scene.

With such a preponderance of rural ridings in the region it is not surprising to find (see figure 1.2) that Atlantic provincial legislatures have lagged behind the rest of Canada in proportions of women elected throughout the past few decades. The shape of the two curves in figure 1.2 is similar; both begin below 5 per cent in the 1960s, rise slowly in the 1970s, more rapidly in the 1980s, and then level off starting in the late

Figure 1.2 Proportions of women in provincial legislatures, Atlantic region and elsewhere in Canada, 1964–2004.

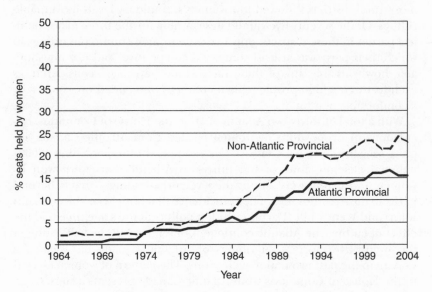

1990s. But the proportion in Atlantic Canada has remained below that in the other provinces throughout the period covered, and the Atlantic pla-teau is near 15 per cent, compared with well over 20 per cent elsewhere.

To see how these lower numbers of women elected relate to rural rid-ings, consider a recent set of elections. All four Atlantic provinces held elections in 2003. The resulting proportions of seats won by women are combined and summarized in table 1.1,[15] where the right-hand column breaks them down according to whether or not the district is in one of the six main urban centres listed above. We find that 27 per cent of the rid-ings in and around these urban centres (13 of 49) were won by women, compared with only 11 per cent (15 of 133) of the more rural ridings.[16] The huge difference between these two proportions is completely in line with the aforementioned statistical models that link low numbers of women elected to higher levels of rurality.

Can we interpret the Atlantic rural deficit in terms of partisan prefer-ences? Table 1.1 also breaks down the 2003 combined provincial election results by party, and a glance at the numbers shows that the answer is no. The Progressive Conservatives won in all four Atlantic provinces, and fared especially well in rural ridings. However, looking along the 'more

Table 1.1 Proportions of seats won by women in Atlantic provincial elections in 2003, in the main urban centres and more rural districts, by political party (total seats won by men and women in parentheses).

Electoral district	Political Party			Rural/urban totals
	NDP	Liberal	PC	
More rural	0% (5)	9% (43)	13% (85)	11% (133)
Urban centres	38% (13)	10% (10)	27% (26)	27% (49)
Party totals	28% (18)	9% (53)	16% (111)	15% (182)

Source: Provincial election archives for the four Atlantic provinces.

rural' row in table 1.1, we see that rural districts that voted Conservative were no less likely to elect women than were rural districts that preferred other parties. Women were elected in 13 per cent of the rural PC ridings, compared with 9 per cent in the rural Liberal ridings, and zero in the rural New Democrat ridings. The rural deficit in Atlantic Canada emerges as a separate and independent electoral pattern that transcends partisan characteristics, just as it does in other regions. Atlantic cities elect substantial numbers of women, just like cities elsewhere do. But that so much of Atlantic Canada is rural means that the more rural ridings dominate, giving a lower overall proportion of women than in other regions.

These quantitative patterns help provide electoral context for the present hands-on investigation of women's leadership in rural Atlantic Canada. As we have seen, the impediments to women's election arise principally in the recruitment and selection processes that occur at the grassroots level. The key unknown in those processes involves the women who would form a pool of potential candidates.

Knowing more about the pool of female potential candidates is crucial for addressing not only the historical reasons for the dearth of women elected, but also practical questions about the future prospects for change in rural women's leadership and what steps might be taken by interested stakeholders to hasten change. A number of existing organizations are taking an active role. Governments typically are considering the impact of policy or regulatory changes on women's leadership. For example, the Rural Secretariat of Canada includes community capacity building and women's empowerment as core elements of its mandate. As another example, the Nova Scotia Advisory Council on the Status of Women operates a campaign school in support of prospective women candidates in that province. Non-partisan organizations such as Feminists for Just and Equitable Public Policy (FemJEPP) and Equal Voice lobby to enhance women's participation in public affairs, including electoral politics. Finally, political parties are going to some length in efforts to improve their public image in regard to women's empowerment. Lynda Erickson observed that as far back as the early 1980s 'party leaders had voiced their support for increasing the number of women candidates, and parties had organized activities designed to do this, including, for example workshops for women interested in party candidacies' (1998, 233). Lisa Young and William Cross found continued support for measures to increase the number of women holding elected office, within the major national parties, with the exception of the Canadian Alliance Party (2003, 106). At the 2003 Liberal Party leadership convention Paul Martin explicitly endorsed the goal of gender parity in parliament and called for Liberal Party actions to help bring this about: 'We have to go out across this country and, in riding after riding, recruit young women who want to dedicate themselves to public service' (cited in Galloway 2003, A5). The effectiveness of all of these organizations' endeavours to increase women's candidacy rests on their familiarity with the pool of potential candidates. However, that familiarity has been extremely limited to date, especially in rural areas. Nova Scotia Lieutenant-Governor Myra Freeman once remarked that 'we really don't know who the women in the [Liberal] Party are outside of the provincial capital.'[17] It goes without saying that non-affiliated rural women leaders are even less visible.

The example of a political party trying to increase the number of female candidates serves as a useful template for formulating some of the most pertinent questions about rural women's leadership and participation in electoral politics. Since candidate recruitment and selection are internal functions of political parties, a party might reasonably expect to be able to effect change more easily than could an outside organization. But party leadership does not control nominations, and it would likely encounter resistance from its local grassroots associations if it tried to exert influence (Carty and Eagles 2005, 85–6). What would be the extent and substance of local resistance to requests from above to recruit more women? Now, suppose that the party and its local members could find common ground on this shared goal. Even if we could inform its strategists of a universal historical cause of the rural deficit, this information would still not be sufficient to guarantee accomplishment of the goal. Are there enough qualified women leaders to supply a substantial increase in the number of rural women candidates for the party to field? Where would the party find them? In other words, what are their occupations, in what public activities have they been involved, and so forth? These questions are crucial if the party is to avoid the pitfalls of assuming 'that the stepping stones into politics are set in concrete' and 'that the stepping stones used by men must also be used by women' (Darcy, Welch, and Clark 1994, 180). Moreover, even if the party could find additional prospects, could it assume that these women want to be recruited? Or would it have to persuade them, and if so, how much reluctance would the party encounter, and on what would this reluctance be based? Finally, would recruitment strategies have to be tailored to the region or, even more locally? In the absence of electoral opportunity over the past decades, we could reasonably expect rural women's leadership to take different trajectories in different regions, as a result of differing political and economic environments. This could affect where to look for the best nominees, as well as what sort of aversions to candidacy would be encountered. These questions have never been addressed, or in some cases even asked, largely because of the difficulty of accessing the pool of potential candidates.

This book presents results from an empirical study which, for the first time, put these very questions to women who are uniquely qualified to address them on the basis of their personal experiences. To carry out this study, I gathered rural community leaders together in small groups throughout the four Atlantic provinces and then interviewed these women about their experiences and perceptions of leadership, public life, and running for elected office. A small number of them are politicians or partisan insiders who could walk into the provincial assembly or party convention and be recognized by name. Others are public service insiders who could walk into a provincial advisory council on the status of women or the Status of Women Canada office and be greeted by name. Some are known at the provincial level in a professional capacity and would be recognized within specific policy communities centred on, say, forestry or education. The rest of the women are local leaders engaged in civic activities on a smaller, usually county-level, stage. Overall, participants in this study are the women who would be in the pool of potential candidates in rural Atlantic ridings, but who, for the most part, are not running.

Insights from women at the centre of action are made all the more valuable by recent studies showing that the most obvious prima facie answers involving traditionalism do not hold up to scrutiny. In their study of regional variations in public opinion on a range of issues related to women's equality, Brenda O'Neill and Lynda Erickson (2003) found that opinion in Atlantic Canada, with two exceptions, is very near the Canadian average. One exception is that Atlantic Canadians definitely and consistently fall on the interventionist side of economic issues. Elsewhere in Canada this orientation is often thought to be favourable to the election of women, via inferred support for the New Democratic Party, which has generally fielded more women candidates than the other major parties have. However, this logical connection breaks down in Atlantic Canada. Historian Margaret Conrad found that 'social democratic leanings in the region have often been expressed in terms of red toryism and left liberalism rather than in NDP support' (2003, 84).[18] The other exception is that more people report being religious in Atlantic Canada than they do elsewhere in Canada. Nevertheless, O'Neill and Erickson found that the associated religious beliefs are not 'feeding a particularly negative nor unique set of attitudes towards women and feminism' (2003, 117). Weighing all of their results, O'Neill and Erickson concluded that 'while opinion in the region provides a perhaps necessary condition for increasing women's political representation, this alone is not sufficient for ensuring that it comes about' (2003, 118). In another study, Joanna Everitt found no evidence of direct or systematic gender bias in media coverage of election campaigns in Atlantic Canada, and she concluded: 'Nor can one argue that the small number of women in provincial legislatures is the result of gender biases in election coverage' (2003, 95). These results suggest that we have to look beyond regional stereotypes to find the real barriers at work and support the proposition that substantive new insight can be gained by consulting directly with women who are involved in public affairs.

The hands-on approach of the present inquiry accesses the intermediate range of political participation spanning from the informal to the formal. Prior work on women's leadership in Atlantic Canada has typically addressed one or the other category exclusively: they have either studied civic engagement in voluntary organizations (George 2000; Neal 1998) or interviewed women who hold elected office (Arscott 1997; Crossley 1997; Desserud 1997; Carbert and Black 2003). Here, we have an assortment of women in all such categories sitting down together to contribute their individual insights, and to interact with one another. As we shall see, the interviews in this study confirm that the deficit in women elected is a symptom of deeper systemic forces that have a particular impact on rural communities and that flow through all aspects of public life therein. After all, running for elected office is not the isolated endeavour of an ambitious individual. Typically, candidates are recruited as part of a team of supporters. The question 'who gets recruited and why?' is really a question of how local hierarchies are formed and perpetuated. Furthermore, electoral ambition cannot be taken for granted. The question 'to what degree are potential female candidates deterred by their own reluctance?' is very much about how women perceive other people's view of them and how they understand local expectations of political representatives. Thus, the act of running, or not running, emanates from a myriad of interpersonal relationships, civic activities, and community dynamics that weave together to form the fabric of public life. These relationships, activities, and dynamics are the real subjects of the interviews and of this book. By situating their own leadership activities and ambitions within this framework, these women tell us a great deal about rural public life, in many ways going beyond their participation in that system.

One nice feature of carrying out this study in rural communities is that all of these relationships, activities, and dynamics are far more transparent than they are in urban settings. This transparency has everything to do with the human scale of civic affairs. Just as people in rural areas can often trace a line of descent from one generation to another through the passage of marriage, divorce, and assorted scandals, so too, can they trace a line of decision-making from one government office to another through the passage of federal-provincial relations and partisan rivalries. People literally see politics happen before their eyes because they know the various players in multiple capacities. Wealth is not anonymous, either, because rural people are more likely than people in urban centres to invest their assets in the physical capital by which they earn a living, for example, a new boat, a new backhoe, or renovations to a shop. Neighbours can usually figure out where the money comes from, how much is spent, and the probability of it being a worthwhile expenditure or not. If public sector money is involved, the allocation and expenditure of funds are all the more likely to become public knowledge. Interviewees attested to a propensity to keep track of this information. By contrast, voters in an urban and highly diversified economy scarcely notice the expenditure of public sector, economic development funds, unless that becomes a major news item, for example, the proposal in 2000 for the national Department of Industry to bail out the Ottawa Senators hockey team when it made the front page of national newspapers. Very few urban expenditures, however large, achieve such notoriety, tucked away as they are in the business pages.

These distinctions resonate in historical accounts of Atlantic Canada. In her survey of the history of women in Atlantic Canada, Suzanne Morton noted that 'anonymity was rare and difficult to maintain even in the region's relatively small cities. In communities where people were likely to know each other, gossip may have been a particular source of power and vulnerability' (2000, 122). Conrad and Hiller characterized Atlantic culture in terms of a 'deep sense of place' (2001, 1), which Morton ascribed to the rural and small-town experience: 'Older and relatively stable populations fostered intense localisms and bonds of community and kinship, that were reinforced by settlement in ethnic and sectarian enclaves' (2000, 122). To Morton, Atlantic Canada has always had 'two distinct realities, one urban and industrial, the other rural and grounded in a resource economy' (2000, 120). She found the greater weight of the latter – demographically and culturally – to be a defining characteristic of the region, which has been the slowest to urbanize in Canada. Conrad and Hiller interpreted this characteristic in terms of the region's position on the periphery of the main engines of economic wealth and prosperity on the North American continent.

That rural voters are specially attuned to their local political scene was confirmed in a study by André Blais and associates (2003, 657–64). The Canada Election Studies team found that in the 2000 national election, rural voters behaved very much like the most sophisticated urban voters in one crucial regard: their propensity to express a preference for the local candidate, not just the party leader. Whereas few but the most politically knowledgeable urban voters would express a local preference, most rural voters did so. This finding is consistent with the notion that rural people, in general, have a keen sense of civic affairs in their own community, probably due to the relative transparency of politics there.[19] For academic research, transparency is priceless.

Even among attuned rural voters, the women interviewed in this study stand out as particularly well positioned to characterize the dynamics of local public life. Many are closely involved enough to have an insider's view of the process, but they do not occupy such high positions of responsibility that they felt obliged to be especially reticent or discreet. In some ways, talking to these women is better than talking to politicians themselves.

Overview of the Book

This book is an intensely local account of political life in the small towns, coastlines, and bush of Atlantic Canada, told from the first-hand perspective of 126 women who are a mainstay of their community's life. It makes abundant use of direct quotations, interspersed with commentary and analysis. Its structure is intended to provide the reader with a genuine understanding of the women's comments and concerns, organized thematically and presented in an accessible manner. First, chapter 2 describes the research process, in which I organized and moderated a series of fourteen in-person group interviews across the four Atlantic provinces, with the assistance of major government and non-government organizations. It explains how the participants were selected and provides brief descriptions of the facilitating organizations. It also describes the format of the meetings and addresses methodological issues associated with the interview technique that was employed. The chapter ends by relating a curious intertwinement of organizations that I discovered while carrying out the fieldwork.

Chapter 3 presents some of the most relevant leadership characteristics of the interviewees, based on their responses to a questionnaire that accompanied the interviews. In addition to straightforward leadership activities such as candidacy and board appointments, it addresses socio-economic resources that are generally recognized as indispensable components of building leadership. Moving beyond objective measures of leadership, chapter 3 reports interviewees' self-appraisals of their own leadership qualities and performance, their personal motivations for participating in public life, their partisan affiliations, and a rough indication of ideological orientations. As well as telling us what the participants have in common, the questionnaire responses reveal the significant diversity that exists among rural women leaders in this region. While it would be presumptuous to claim to know these women in any personal or overall sense, this information on their leadership characteristics forms a solid basis for interpreting their insights and reflections on public life.

Chapter 4 examines images of leadership – the interviewees' subjective and personal perceptions of leadership, in the abstract. It presents their views of what a leader should look like, identifies whom they particularly admire and wish to emulate, and discusses their perceptions of the experiences of prominent women who have achieved high levels of power. Their reflections on images of leadership tell us a good deal about the psychological frames of reference that these women bring to their own political participation and through which they filter their personal experiences in their communities.

Chapters 5 through 7 delve further into those experiences, structured in terms of overarching themes that emerged from the discussions. No two interview groups were the same, either in composition or content;

nevertheless, the undeniable pattern that emerged from the interviews was a persistent commonality of themes and concerns that crossed provincial, ethnic, class, and partisan lines. In one form or another, the discussions conveyed the sense that politics does not exist as a sphere separate from other important components of life. Interviewees at one meeting after another brought forth concerns about overlaps between politics and their family life, between politics and their own occupations, and between politics and the overall local economy. The dominance of these concerns led me to generalize, as can be seen by the chapter titles, on Sharon Sutherland's marvellous metaphor of 'slushy intersections' – the messy and imprecisely defined overlap of activities that we might wish were independent but in reality are not (2001, 10).

Chapter 5 reports the interviewees' perceptions of the interaction between family life and their civic involvement. High expectations of family involvement obviously introduce the potential for gender-role constraints on how much time women have available for leadership activities outside the home. The chapter begins by outlining interviewees' assessments of how onerous are the responsibilities of a rural politician and to what extent they themselves have been deterred by the prospect of time conflicts with their family responsibilities. It then moves beyond straightforward gender-role constraints, to illustrate how families present burdens other than time demands. Quite a few participants conceptualized their families as a sort of corporate unit, in the sense that their individual successes and failures are shared by, and reflect on, all of their family members. This discussion leads naturally into the conventional Atlantic stereotype of the 'family vote,' as an extension of familial loyalty. Participants brought up the prevalence of family legacies of power and influence. In some cases the legacy involved sons effectively inheriting their father's elected seats; in others it involved behind-the-scenes influence wielded by wealthy families who were referred to as 'overseers.'

Chapter 6 discusses some of the ways in which these women perceived their jobs as affecting their participation in public affairs and their own political aspirations. It begins by showing that the conventional prohibition against the partisan participation of public sector employees is far from dead, despite the repeal of formal legal prohibitions. Interviewees' comments revealed a surprising depth and breadth of adherence to this as an underlying guiding principle. Teachers are a notable exception, and some of the implications of their comparative freedom are explored. There were extensive discussions surrounding the impact of private sector occupations on political activities and ambitions. Separate descriptions are presented in the (often counterintuitive) comments regarding small-business owners, large publicly owned corporations that are involved in resource extraction, and mid-sized locally owned businesses with substantial numbers of employees.

Chapter 7 examines a pervasive uneasiness among rural women leaders about how politics overlaps with the local economy. It describes participants' disapproval of aspects of local public life that go beyond individual-level characteristics, as they grappled with the large-scale forces that buffet the entire community. In one discussion group after another interviewees initiated and carried on intense discussions about how public funds are distributed in their communities and the profound consequences for their own electoral ambitions. Much of the disapproval centred on the administration of economic development programs that are ostensibly aimed at encouraging and providing the infrastructure for the growth of local businesses. This chapter begins by illustrating the pervasive feeling of distaste for politics that was shared by a surprisingly high proportion of the interviewees. It then moves on to substantive critiques of patronage practices, including old familiar practices from the past, some of which persist, as well as new ones that have arisen as the political and economic environments have evolved. This topic is nuanced, in that many interviewees recognized the important role that a conscientious patron plays in communities with fragile economies, and they weighed the potential for good against the potential to sustain further long-term collective harm. The chapter ends by presenting the views of some participants – mostly the more affluent ones – who have shied away from politics out of fear of being maligned by what they see as an undue backlash against patronage. This curiously converse relationship is illustrated by the interaction between women on both sides of the fence.

Chapter 8 concludes this book with an analytic synthesis that attempts to contextualize and interpret the results of the interviews and questionnaire. It outlines structural features of rural Atlantic Canada that underpin the dynamics of public life, as highlighted in the interviews, and the strong influence they exert on these women's ambitions and leadership activities. In developing this analysis, the chapter weaves together some of the most important results presented earlier. The overall synthesis is used to highlight opportunities and obstacles to the election of more women in the Atlantic region and to consider points of comparison and contrast with other locations elsewhere in Canada.

The 126 women interviewed here are themselves important players in the political landscape of rural Atlantic Canada. Their activities have helped to shape that landscape. Their decisions about their future involvement will have significant ramifications, including, but not restricted to, the numbers of women elected to political office. Therefore, what these women had to say is directly relevant to the political dynamics of the region and more than merely representative or symbolic. This book focuses squarely on the women interviewed, on their leadership goals and aspirations, and on their understanding of public life in their communities, as presented from their own points of view and their own experiences.

2 An Interview Series in Atlantic Canada

To carry out the study as described in the introduction, I organized and moderated a series of fourteen discussion groups across the four Atlantic provinces, which involved interviewing 126 rural women community leaders over an eight-month period in 2000. Seven of the meetings were held in Nova Scotia, two in New Brunswick, one in Prince Edward Island, and four in the province of Newfoundland and Labrador. Two were held in areas that have a strong Acadian presence and included bilingual participants. Each community that I visited had a population of fewer than 20,000 inhabitants, and most were much smaller than that. While population provides a straightforward quantitative categorization, it can sometimes be misleading about the nature of a given community. For example, some small towns are bedroom communities for adjacent urban centres. Others have come into existence only recently, or feature transient populations, and thereby lack the transparency and stability (described in the introduction) that characterize much of Atlantic Canada. All of the communities visited in the course of this project go back many generations and feature relatively stable populations, and none are adjacent to large urban centres.

The range of geographical locations encompassed a good deal of economic diversity, as the various communities were economically dominated by (usually one of) a number of resource extraction industries – farming, fisheries, forestry, mining – and, to a lesser extent, tourism. While the economic fortunes of the different communities varied somewhat, it is safe to say that none were stellar. Conrad and Hiller documented an economic decline throughout the Atlantic region since the second half of the nineteenth century and associated it with long-term patterns of high unemployment, no large-scale immigration after 1850, and out-migration of young people. In the twentieth century, the 1990s, in particular, were a difficult decade for Atlantic Canada because three independent factors converged: The general declines in commodity prices during the 1990s were especially hard on the resource-based economies of rural areas; an ecological crisis in the fisheries compounded long-standing structural unemployment; and the national (Liberal) government carried out a vigourous program of budget cutting, aimed at balancing the national budget. The high dependence of the Atlantic provinces on transfers from Ottawa meant that the cutbacks had a disproportionately negative impact on them (House 1999, 249). The interviews were carried out within what can therefore be described as a fragile economic environment.

Arranging the Interviews

The meetings were arranged with the assistance of major government and non-governmental organizations. In each case I followed a series of contacts until a meeting could be organized that would satisfy the research criteria. Ideally, this required only two steps: I would describe my project requirements to an official at the main office of a selected organization, and this official would direct me to a local person of some stature in the rural community under consideration, who might be willing to facilitate such an event. The recruitment process began when I contacted this local facilitator and asked her to identify eight local women who, in her opinion, had demonstrated leadership capacity and who would be willing to participate in a group interview about public life and personally running for elected office. The facilitator was specifically asked to consider all types of leadership, and to *not* select interviewees preferentially on the basis of experience in electoral politics, because a central goal of this project was to gain insight into why qualified women are not running for elected office. In most cases the facilitator also arranged for, or suggested, a venue for the meeting. Typically, only about two-weeks' lead time was required to set up the event, and arrangements fell into place with remarkable ease.

This approach to interviewee recruitment was designed to access the entire range of politically active women in particular rural communities. Without the help of a local facilitator, it would have been very difficult to identify many of the women who participanted in this project, because the behind-the-scenes political activity of some key players is often invisible to the world at large. Relying on lists and formal records would have resulted in a set of participants with a much narrower range of experi-

ences in public life. By seeking out local knowledge during the recruitment process, each group meeting captured the unity of a single political
scene with a diverse range of participants.

The topic of the project – rural women's leadership – seems to have
contributed to the success of recruitment. At one meeting, a high school
principal related that she had been feeling tired and was not going to
attend, but she pulled herself together partly out of curiosity to see who
else had been invited. Even more striking was how avidly participants
seized on to the designation 'rural woman leader,' judging by how often
an interviewee used this phrase in referring to herself. As a general rule,
people tend to balk at being labelled, so it seems fair to say that the categorization used here is a meaningful one that resonated with the participants' self-image.

As part of my attempt to access the diversity of political life in Atlantic
Canada, I contacted a wide range of organizations with very different
mandates and memberships. As detailed below, eleven meetings were
arranged through non-partisan organizations and three through political parties. The project began with the Nova Scotia Advisory Council on
the Status of Women. Under the direction of executive director Brigitte
Neumann, each of the three regional fieldworkers employed by the
Advisory Council facilitated a meeting in a rural community within her
region. As a provincial government agency, the council has access to substantial resources, and it provided government boardrooms (complete
with refreshments) in which to conduct sessions.

In Halifax the Canadian Research Institute for the Advancement for
Women (CRIAW) suggested that I contact Women's FishNet, a set of
loosely affiliated groups that sprang up to speak for women's interests
during the crisis in the east coast cod fishery in the early 1990s. FishNet
dealt with the implementation of the Atlantic Groundfish Strategy
(TAGS) program to buy out fishers after the 1995 moratorium on the cod
fishery. Later, the agenda of FishNet expanded beyond the fisheries to
activities relating to the economic restructuring of coastal areas, such as
dissemination of information about government retraining programs.

Soon after meeting with the FishNet group, an opportunity arose to
meet with the Business Women's Association (BWA) in the same county.
The association is an informal group of women that meet semi-regularly
for breakfast. This session provided an interesting counterpoint to the
FishNet session because it comprised women in the same county, but
closer to the centre of local power. In fact, some of the BWA women had
been the subject of conversation at the meeting with FishNet.

The Federated Women's Institutes (WI) of Nova Scotia, Prince

Edward Island, and Newfoundland each arranged for a meeting to be held with executive members in their respective province. Since 1896 the WI (known in Quebec as Cercles des Fermières) has been Canada's most important rural women's organization, sheerly in terms of its size and scope, with remarkably little disruption in its mandate and organizational structure. It has historically been closely associated with the extension divisions of provincial departments of agriculture, and it can still be characterized by its original mandate to improve the overall quality of rural life (Black and Brandt 1999; Carbert 1995; Halpern 2001; Kechnie 2003). Newfoundland is an exception, as farming was less important there economically. In that province the WI descends from the Jubilee Guilds, established in 1934 for the purpose of promoting the production and sale of traditional handicrafts.

One meeting was facilitated by the Women's Community-based Economic Development (CED) Network of Nova Scotia, a non-profit, non-governmental organization launched in 1997 through the Women for Economic Equality Society, itself a non-profit organization founded in 1996. Earlier policies promoting economic development relied on large-scale infusions of investment capital, often from foreign sources, in industrial and manufacturing enterprises producing for export markets. Community economic development is oriented towards micro-enterprises and cooperative ventures that produce goods and services for local consumption. Instead of focusing narrowly on the profitability of individual firms, community economic development focuses on the overall sustainability of business operations in particular cultural and environmental contexts. The underlying rationale is that the social cohesion of a community is an essential element in the economic environment in which individual enterprises succeed or fail. For its part, the Women's CED Network employs local coordinators to organize support groups for women, mount short-term skills workshops, and help women to identify economic opportunities and develop business plans.

While the Newfoundland Advisory Council on the Status of Women does not employ regional fieldworkers, its president, Joyce Hancock, was able to refer me to the Women in Resource Development Committee, a non-government organization that does hire regional fieldworkers, who were able to assist me. The WRDC was formed in 1997 with the mandate of increasing women's labour force participation as skilled-trades workers in the province's new offshore oil and gas industry. At the time of my interviews, WRDC was in the midst of mounting a twenty-four-week program called Orientation to Trades and Technology, offered annually at regional campuses of the College of the North Atlantic, in preparation for admission to a formal apprenticeship program. Recruitment was aimed at small groups of women, who were expected to form self-help groups.[1] As with the Women's CED Network of Nova Scotia, the WRDC's goals include women's empowerment and integration into community decision-making processes.

The New Brunswick Advisory Council on the Status of Women does not employ regional fieldworkers either; however, its staff referred me to an appointed member who lives in a rural area. This council member facilitated a meeting in an English-speaking enclave on the Acadian coast where the Liberal Party has traditionally been dominant in both national and provincial elections.

To balance Liberal strength on the Acadian coast of New Brunswick, an interview meeting was held on the English-speaking and Loyalist Fundy coast where the Conservatives have traditionally been dominant. This session was facilitated by an official with the federal Conservatives, who is from the area. Two meetings in Newfoundland were also facilitated by political parties, one by the Provincial Liberals and another by the provincial Conservatives.

Interview Format

The meetings were conducted in English and lasted approximately two hours. On arrival at the designated location, respondents sat down at a boardroom table and filled out consent forms. I introduced myself and the project with a five-minute presentation, which included graphs comparing historical proportions of women elected in different regions of Canada. I ended by framing the discussion that was to follow in terms of the general question of why so few women find their way to elected office in rural Atlantic Canada. A visual device, involving images designed to capture conventional gender stereotypes, was used as an ice-breaker exercise by which participants introduced themselves. To get the open-ended part of the interview started, I asked one or more specific questions about the local community. The ensuing discussions typically engaged multiple interviewees in animated conversations, interspersed by questions and prompts from me.

The interviewees proved to be exceptionally articulate and enthusiastic. That they were sophisticated and actively engaged with the subject contributed a great deal to the success of the open-ended interviews. Participants could, and did, bring their own issues to the table, regardless of whether I had anticipated their importance during the research design. This flexibility enabled the emergence of some of the most valuable insights reported in subsequent chapters. It also allowed participants to dispel misconceptions that I had brought to the project.[2]

The discussions were videotaped and later transcribed to written text. More than twenty hours of interviews constitutes a rich source of information about rural women's leadership in Atlantic Canada. The excerpts provided in this book comprise but a fraction of the transcripts. They were selected for being relevant to the topic, representative of the discussion from which they were extracted, and of similar discussions in other groups, while at the same time being articulate, concise, and self-contained. Preference was given to excerpts in which participants were speaking on the basis of first-hand experience. Care was taken in selecting them, in an attempt to impart a clear sense of the discussions, while preserving their integrity. Care was also taken to keep the identity of the interviewees confidential.

At the end of a discussion, participants were asked to fill out an anonymous written questionnaire that asked about their experience in electoral politics, civic engagement, partisanship, and basic sociodemographic situation. It also asked them to assess their motivations for participating in public life and to make a self-appraisal of their leadership qualities and performance. Of the 126 interviewees, all but one completed the questionnaire (99 per cent).

A $50 honorarium was offered to each participant to offset travel and other expenses incurred in attending the meeting. The honorarium helped to reinforce the professional credibility of the project and to convey an appreciation for the contributions of the participants. A few individuals, and one entire group, donated their honoraria to a local women's shelter or other organization. Two women (an elected official and an employee of a non-profit organization) declined the honorarium to avoid what they saw as a 'conflict-of-interest,' in that attending the meeting might be seen to be part of their regular job responsibilities.

The interview format had much in common with what is referred to as a focus group, and some of the methodological research about focus groups applies here as well. Focus-group interviews are appropriate for research that examines in depth a single topic with selected individuals from smaller and more specific segments of society than would be captured in mass population surveys. This technique has been characterized as a 'research method that is respectful and not condescending to your target audience' (Morgan and Krueger, cited in Morgan 2002, 142). This is obviously an important attribute in the present study, which deals with women who have achieved a good deal and have variously received much or little recognition for it.

One common concern is that for many people the office boardroom setting so typical of focus-group interviews feels sterile and artificial. Indeed, this project adhered to that formula: four meetings were held in government-office boardrooms to which facilitators had access through their jobs; another four were held in the boardroom of a non-governmental organization, and five in a restaurant private-meeting room that had a boardroomlike table. The remaining meeting was held in a participant's home. But what is sterile and artificial for some people can be comfortable and familiar for others. When I assembled several community leaders around a boardroom table in their own community, it was not markedly different from many other occasions when they would have been in the same room, around the same table, and in some cases with the same people, for a committee meeting or other such business of public life. In short, the interview setting was familiar and comfortable for the interviewees in this study, and the topic under discussion centred on what they usually do in that same setting.

While the moderator has an important role to play, the composition of a focus group largely determines the quality of discussion. In addition to the individual qualifications of the participants in this study to speak on women's leadership, how they interacted with each other was also important. Gender has been cited as an important element in determining the extent to which participants are willing to express an unconventional opinion and the extent to which they 'disclose' or reveal important information about themselves. As a general rule, of the various male-female combinations, women disclose the most information to women moderators in an all-female group (Fern 2001, 35–8) – the same combination as used here.

Group interviews are especially effective if cohesion inside the group supports individuals in a way that allows them to express anxiety-provoking and socially unpopular ideas freely in the spontaneous flow of discussion (Fern 2001, 102; Stewart and Shamdasani 1990, 38). The groups assembled here were cohesive in various ways, with a good number of participants being friends, relatives, and/or colleagues. Groups in which a level of intimacy had already been established often produced the most penetrating discussions, for example, a frank discussion analysing why a participant's run for the PC Party nomination had failed. As moderator, I felt enabled to push and probe respondents beyond conventional platitudes because they were securely embedded on their home turf, supported by their friends and associates.

Focus groups work best when participants talk about what they have in common because they 'benefit from group interaction and the resultant social pressures from other group members any time the phenomenon under study is "collective" in nature' (Fern 2001, 114–15, 128). This project was precisely about what the participants had in common. Civic engagement, including political recruitment, is inherently a 'collective' phenomenon. Fundamentally, the unit of analysis here is the local political system, and participants were speaking about their shared experience of that system.

One potential risk that seems applicable to this study is that high-status individuals often cause friction in focus groups because they seek to monopolize the floor, to distinguish themselves or to secure respect from other participants (Fern 2001, 18; Greenbaum 2000, 180). This problem did arise during part of one meeting, the transcript of which became indecipherable for brief periods, due to competing voices and cutting asides. Other than this one time with this one group, however, the problem did not arise, in spite of the presence of high-status individuals at several other meetings. For the most part, participants exhibited a clear sense of 'who defers to whom' in an established hierarchy. Contrary to what might have been expected, this sense of hierarchy often produced a pleasant and constructive dynamic, for example, when two older participants prodded and cajoled a younger woman who had been designated as a possible candidate before her admiring supporters.

Finally, the interview format presents the potential to seek generalizations beyond Atlantic Canada, keeping in mind the risks with which extrapolation is fraught. One of the strengths of in-depth, open-ended interviews is the opportunity to get to know the interviewees quite well in regard to the topic at hand, perhaps well enough to formulate a theoretical understanding that may be generalizable. To this end, chapters 3 through 7 look intensively at the interviewees themselves, probing into the local context of their experiences and listening to what they feel has influenced their perceptions of leadership, public life, and running for elected office. Then, by synthesizing these results in the context of regional characteristics, chapter 8 takes a step towards an understanding of their leadership in terms of larger structural contours in the social, political, and economic environment. The particular experiences and perceptions belong uniquely to the women interviewed, of course. Yet the underlying structures, and their consequences for women's leadership, can sensibly be compared and contrasted with those in other parts of Canada.

Organizational Inter-twinement

A striking pattern emerged in carrying out the inquiries to arrange the meetings. As already described, I employed multiple, independent points of access, including government bodies, political parties, women's shelters, development organizations, and so on. But no matter where I started my inquiries in a given geographical area, I often found that the different series of contacts led me to different people who were connected in one way or another to the same central group of women who occupied multiple positions in a few government and non-governmental organizations, usually in the capital city. In Newfoundland, for example, I approached Barbara Neis, a professor at Memorial University, on the basis of her involvement with the Newfoundland FishNet. Neis referred me to the WRDC, on whose board she sits. Neis is among several FishNet organizers in Newfoundland who had gravitated towards WRDC as the implementation of the TAGS program wound down. In a separate inquiry, I approached Joyce Hancock on the basis of her job as president of the Newfoundland Advisory Council on the Status of Women. She also referred me to the WRDC and informed me that she was a founding member and co-chair of the WRDC board. When I approached the Progressive Conservative Party of Newfoundland to facilitate a meeting, I was referred to the president of the PC Women's Association, who, I learned later, is also employed as a WRDC fieldworker. In the meeting arranged in conjunction with the Liberal Party of Newfoundland, one of the participants was teaching a course in the WRDC's Orientation to Trades and Technology program, and she invited me to speak to her self-help group. At another meeting, there was a woman who had worked on a proposal for overall WRDC funding; at yet another, someone who sits on the WRDC board of directors. Thus, the WRDC had an unanticipated reach and scope across the entire province.

The prominence of this non-government organization can arguably be related to its role in the government's policy agenda and the connections that its organizers bring to the endeavour. The WRDC Orientation to Trades and Technology program is one component of the Labour Market Development Agreement and the Canada–Newfoundland Offshore Agreement that was signed between the governments of Canada and Newfoundland in 1999. It receives funding from Status of Women Canada,

Newfoundland Human Resources and Employment, and most substantially, Human Resources Development Canada. Joyce Hancock, its founding member and co-chair, as well as president of the provincial Advisory Council on the Status of Women also sits on the Premier's Council on Social Development. One WRDC board member is employed as director of research and planning for the Women's Policy Office of the government of Newfoundland and Labrador. Another is employed as an employment equity consultant with HRDC in St John's. Yet another is an administrator at the College of the North Atlantic. The private sector is also represented on the WRDC board. One board member is an employee of the Iron Ore Company of Canada and has been appointed to provincial equity boards. Another is a researcher for the Canadian Auto Workers union, representing fish-plant workers. It seems that the WRDC has elements of a flexible, project-driven corporatist arrangement.[3]

The Women's CED Network played a similar role in Nova Scotia. When fieldworkers employed by the Nova Scotia Advisory Council on the Status of Women were asked to identify community leaders for my interviews, their lists included CED coordinators. As the Newfoundland FishNet organizers gravitated to WRDC when TAGS ended, so too did the key players in Nova Scotia FishNet resurface as initiators of the Women's CED Network. Like the WRDC in Newfoundland, the Women's CED Network in Nova Scotia has a prominence that would seem to go beyond that of a typical grassroots organization. It is supported financially by Nova Scotia Economic Development and Tourism, the Nova Scotia Advisory Council on the Status of Women, Status of Women Canada, HRDC, and the Atlantic Canada Opportunities Agency (ACOA). The network was formally structured as a project operated by another organization called Women for Economic Equality, on whose governing board sat women holding paid employment and appointed positions within the provincial government.

The convergence that I stumbled across in my inquiries demonstrates what a small world it is at the top of these intertwined organizations. In a rural setting, it is difficult to maintain distinctions between government, non-government, and partisan organizations because the same people swim in a fluid sea of activities that ebb and flow with the shifting tides of government funding opportunities. The women who run these organizations are opportunists, in the best sense of that word, as informal networks coalesce around government priorities. Those government priorities, moreover, are to some degree identified in consultation with these same organizers. Given the relatively sparse populations of rural

Atlantic Canada, and even sparser numbers of female professionals who administer the infrastructure of postsecondary education, economic development programs, and political parties, it is almost inevitable that they would occupy multiple and overlapping positions. These women know each other through long-standing networks of personal ties and their current institutional positions – as coordinator, regional field-worker, or board director – were to some extent incidental. By making multiple independent inquiries, I thus encountered an interrelated nexus of 'gender and development' programs funded principally by HRDC, Status of Women Canada, ACOA, and the provincial women's advisory councils.

3 Leadership Characteristics of the Interviewees

Before we can interpret what the interviewees in this study had to say, we should learn who they are, at least in regard to the topic at hand. This study interviewed women who were selected on the basis of their specialized leadership characteristics. Most of them occupy what can be described as a mezzanine level of political participation. While few of them are well-known public figures who are widely recognized on the provincial or national level, it is equally true that they are distinct from the general population, based on the discriminating selection process. What distinguishes them, and how much variation is there among them?

This chapter describes some of the most relevant leadership characteristics of the interviewees, based on responses to a questionnaire. In addition to examining direct measures such as candidacy and board appointments, some of the socioeconomic resources that are generally considered to be the basic building blocks of leadership are also discussed. In an attempt to get at the more subjective components of leadership, the results of questions asking respondents to appraise their own leadership qualities and performance are reported, as are their personal motivations for participating in public life. Finally, responses to standard questions on partisanship and ideology give a sense of how well the study covered the diversity of ideological approaches that different leaders bring to their civic engagement. The information presented here about the leadership characteristics of these women provides the basis for analysing their insights and reflections on public life in subsequent chapters.

I begin by attempting to provide a straightforward answer to the central methodological question: What makes the participants in this study leaders? Chapter 2 describes how the interviewees were selected, that is, how leaders were sought out, but it does not tell us how successful this process was. The questionnaire helps to address this issue. Compiling the responses to several questions reveals that of the 125 interviewees who answered the questionnaire 119 (95 per cent) satisfied at least one of the following criteria:

1. has run or been suggested as a candidate in an election;
2. has served as an appointed member of an official government board in the preceding two years;
3. has worked on an election campaign;
4. serves as an officer in a voluntary organization;
5. regularly performs volunteer work for two or more voluntary organizations.

Of those 119 women, 113 (95 per cent) satisfied one or more of the first four (stronger) criteria, and 107 (90 per cent) satisfied more than one criterion. The one participant who did not answer the questionnaire is a mayor; the six who did not meet any of these criteria were scattered among six different groups. Possibly these six women are leaders in some other (unspecified) manner, but they likely represent a small minority (less than 5 per cent) of outliers who did not fit into the design of the study. All of the groups had at least one exceptional leader, and often several, who satisfied four of the criteria and who contributed a great deal to the discussions. At a minimum, it can be concluded that the overwhelming majority of the interviewees, and all of those quoted in this book, are community leaders, according to any reasonable definition of that term.

Participation in Electoral Politics

The women interviewed in this study reported extensive experience in electoral politics. Beginning with the most visible form of participation, twenty-one (17 per cent) had been candidates for elected political office, and a further fifty-six (44 per cent) had had someone suggest that they stand as candidates but had not run in the election. Thus, a total of seventy-seven of the 126 interviewees (61 per cent) had been at least suggested candidates for election. This proportion speaks to how the participants are perceived as leaders in their own communities. The group discussions described in the following chapters shed light on why some of the fifty-six women chose not to run for election, and why others tried to but had not been nominated.

Some of the twenty-one candidates had run for more than one office, so that the total number of candidacies was thirty-three. The dates of candidacy reach back as far as 1973, with a few in the 1980s; but most were in the 1990s, as could be reasonably expected from the overall trends across Canada (depicted in figure 1.1). Of the thirty-three candidacies, none was at the national level. Five women had been candidates at the provincial level: two of them had been elected, and one of these two had served in cabinet. Eight interviewees had been mayoralty candidates: three of them had been elected. Of fourteen participants who had stood as candidates for municipal councils, nine had been elected. Seven of the women had run for their school boards, and all but one of them had been elected. None of the participants had run for a county-level office such as warden or reeve.

Candidacy is only the tip of the iceberg in terms of participation in electoral politics. During an election campaign, many volunteers perform the bulk of the work, particularly at the national and provincial levels. Of the 125 participants who completed the written questionnaire, seventy-three (58 per cent) had worked on an election campaign, most in more than one capacity. Figure 3.1 identifies their campaign activities. It shows that forty-eight women had done canvassing; forty-two had served as a poll clerk, scrutineer, or other election official; thirty-eight had done campaign administration and office work, including the job of campaign manager; thirty-two had donated money to an election campaign; and twenty-one had performed other miscellaneous tasks such as speech writing, public relations, fundraising, and driving. It is notable that thirty participants had worked on federal election campaigns, even though none had stood as candidates at that level. More than half of the campaign volunteer work reported was for either national or provincial elections, presumably because the campaigns are larger at these higher levels.

In addition to questions on their electoral participation to date, participants were asked about their preferred level of elected office for a future or hypothetical candidacy. Among 125 respondents, sixty-seven (54 per cent) reported that they would prefer the municipal level (mayor, town council, or school board); thirty-one (25 per cent) selected the provincial legislature as their highest preferred level, and thirteen (10 per cent) the House of Commons. This distribution conforms to the commonly cited 'the higher, the fewer' pyramid of political participation, in which more people seek out power where it is most accessible. Fourteen of the women refused to select any of these levels, even in the hypothetical case, indicating a strong aversion to candidacy. Interview discussions described in

Figure 3.1 Interviewees' election campaign activities (73 of 125 were involved with one or more campaigns).

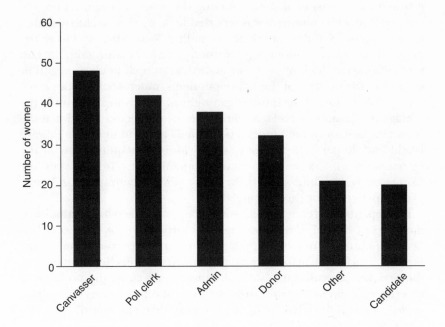

other chapters help to explain this aversion and reveal that, when moving from the hypothetical to actual candidacy, it is not restricted to these fourteen participants. This result, along with the finding that many interviewees had been asked to run in elections, suggests that external barriers are not the only important factors keeping women from elected office in rural Atlantic Canada.

Non-electoral Participation

The women in this study are actively involved in a range of voluntary non-electoral organizations. Volunteer work is an important element of leadership, in that volunteers invest energy, money, and time in their community when they engage in face-to-face interactions with other people. Not all of these interactions are warm and supportive. Much of what is included in civic engagement could be characterized as manipulation or even petty squabbling, which makes a person's willingness to volunteer and hold office without compulsion or reward all the more remarkable.

The study questionnaire included a standardized list of organizations and asked respondents to indicate in which ones they were currently involved (see Verba et al. 1995). Among the types of organizations, the greatest level of involvement was reported to be in 'service club or fraternal organization' (56 respondents, including 30 as officers). Other frequent choices were 'business, professional, farm organization,' 'group with religious affiliation,' and 'social services in such fields as health or services to the needy.' Of the 125 respondents, ninety-four (75 per cent) are volunteers in one or more organizations. This is nearly double the average for Atlantic Canada. A 1997 survey of the region found that the volunteer rate for women ranged between 37 per cent in Prince Edward Island and 40 per cent in Nova Scotia.[1] Moreover, quite a few of the interviewees are volunteers for several organizations: fully seventy-one (57 per cent) do volunteer work for two or more organizations and forty-five (36 per cent) for three or more.

Participants also reported extensive experience in serving as appointed members of official government boards; forty-seven (38 per cent) had been appointed to one or more such boards in the preceding two years. Figure 3.2 shows that at the time twenty women were on education boards; thirteen were on cultural, historical, or tourism boards; and twelve were on economic development boards. A variety of other boards were represented; some of the participants are on more than one board.

Education

Without requiring that the people in charge of our government institutions be demonstrably superior in every regard, it is indisputable that they must have basic administrative and interpersonal skills. In advanced, postindustrial societies, public affairs have become quite complex, in that diverse and multifaceted interests must (at least appear to) be represented and arbitered. As the level of education has risen in the general population, so too have expectations of public officials. Politicians are expected to have sufficient knowledge, sensitivity, and skill to make prudent judgments about the public good. Whichever discipline is pursued, education provides the basic skills of reading, writing, analysis, and numeracy. The ability to synthesize information from a variety of sources, formulate a logical position, and present it persuasively is the basic stuff of power in a liberal democracy. Large-scale quantitative studies have consistently found education to be the single best predictor of political involvement (see, e.g., Verba 1995, chapt. 15).

Figure 3.2 Interviewees' appointed to official government boards, by sector (47 of 125 were on one or more boards).

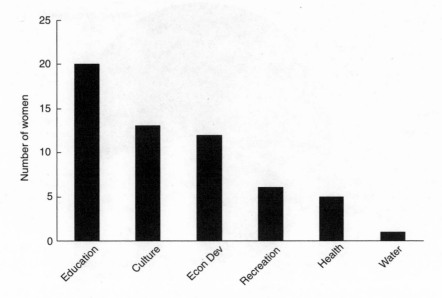

Participants in this study definitely expressed an appreciation of the impact of education in their community. One discussion group decided that the stereotypical distinction between locals in a rural community and 'come-from-aways' misses the point:

> I think the boundary lies between those who were born and lived all their life in [the] county and never got outside of the borders of [the province] and the other side, where you either come from away and fall in love with the community, or you were born here, went away, and came back with new ideas and fresh enthusiasm. And there always seems to be this kind of rift.

This interviewee, like many others, finds that the crucial distinction lies in the education or professional training that people obtain outside the local community.

The study questionnaire asked that participants record their highest level of education (see figure 3.3). Fully 83 per cent of the respondents (103 of 124 who answered this question) had attended a postsecondary institution. Seventy-five of these women (60 per cent) have at least one

Figure 3.3 Interviewees' education status (highest level attained, $n = 124$).

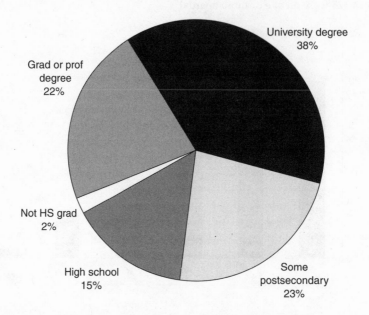

Grad or prof
degree
22%

University degree
38%

Not HS grad
2%

High school
15%

Some
postsecondary
23%

postsecondary degree, of whom twenty-seven (22 per cent) have gradu-
ate or professional degrees.

Data from Canada's 1996 Census (Statistics Canada) help to put these
education levels into perspective. The Census asked respondents to
indicate their highest level of education, with 'university' being the
most advanced option available. Figure 3.4 shows the proportion of the
working-age population of Atlantic Canada that has university as their
highest level of education. This proportion ranges from a low of 12 per
cent in Burin–St George's to a high of 18 per cent in New Brunswick
Southwest. As further context, figure 3.4 also shows this proportion for
the largest urban centre in the region, Halifax (47 per cent), and for all
of Canada (23 per cent). While the Census figures are not directly comparable with this study's questionnaire, in terms of educational categories[2] and age distribution, it is obvious that the interviewees are highly
educated relative both to their own local populations in particular and to
Canada in general.

The husbands of the eighty-seven participants who are married are
also well educated, but not as highly educated as their wives.[3] Of the

Figure 3.4 Percentage of population (age, >15 years) with university as their highest level of education, Statistics Canada 1996, – Canada, Halifax, and selected Atlantic electoral districts.

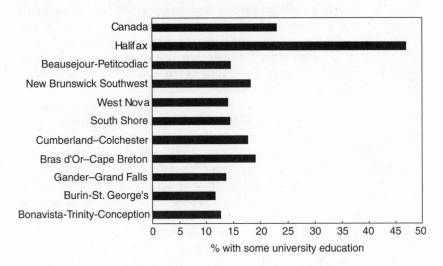

% with some university education

eighty-six husbands whose education was reported, forty-eight (56 per cent) had attended a postsecondary institution, compared with 83 per cent of the interviewees. The education gap between spouses is transparently a product of the interviewee selection process. The focus on those with leadership characteristics directly selected particularly well-educated women and only indirectly selected well-educated husbands, through their choice of spouse. In addition to selection considerations, an education gap is not unusual for rural men where fishers and farmers are likely to operate small enterprises for which no formal education credentials are required. Educated women, such as those interviewed here, often are living in the country because of the careers of the men they marry and less often for their own job opportunities.

Experience that comes with age counts in politics. The age distribution of interviewees is shown in table 3.1 (second-from-the-bottom row). Interviewees were between twenty-five and seventy-eight years of age, with a median (and mean) age of forty-eight, and with more women near the middle than at the extremes. In terms of stereotypical political careers, one might characterize the interviewee of median age as having recently passed by or taken up her prime moments of opportunity for entering electoral politics. In any case, she would plausibly have done some thinking about issues related to this decision during the preceding years. But forty-eight is not necessarily too late to start. It must be remembered that women's political careers tend to get going later than men's do, often being delayed by child-care responsibilities. Many of the women who were younger than the median age were flexing their muscles in terms of community influence and beginning to think about future possibilities. Some of the older women were able to reflect upon decades of either illustrious or unrecognized service.

One might expect that education level would be higher among the younger interviewees than the older ones, because of the massive expansion in the postsecondary system over the past thirty years or so. However, this is not the case. Table 3.1 shows the distribution of participants' education levels across age categories. The raw numbers do not present an obvious pattern of age dependence. Within each age category, all but a few of the women went beyond high school. By assigning numerical values to the education categories, it is possible to calculate a rough average level for each age category, and this mean value is displayed in the bottom row of table 3.1.[4] For every age category, it is between 'some postsecondary' and 'graduated postsecondary.'[5] The main pattern is one of consistently high levels of education across all age groups, with the large majority in all age groups having at least some postsecondary education and most holding degrees. Education has definitely been an important factor in women's involvement in public affairs in Atlantic Canada for generations.

Employment

A cursory reading of this chapter so far might give the mistaken impression of intelligent, but bored women filling their time by volunteering for various local causes. The results, however, show that this is not so. The participants in this study are well employed, especially relative to their neighbours, and their jobs do not get in the way of their high level of civic engagement.

Participants were asked to report their main occupation, by filling in a blank. Of the 125 respondents to the questionnaire, 113 answered this question[6] (see figure 3.5). The most striking result is that more than half of the interviewees reported their occupation as being in the public sector (clockwise from the top in the pie graph). This represents a huge overrepresentation of public sector women in leadership roles, consider-

Table 3.1 Interviewees' education status, by age group (n)

Education level	Age (years)					Total (n)
	25–34	35–44	45–54	55–64	65+	
1 Some high school			2			2
2 Graduated high school	2	3	5	5	2	17
3 Some postsecondary	1	8	7	7	3	26
4 Graduated postsecondary	13	12	11	6	3	45
5 Graduated professional/graduate school	2	5	7	4	5	23
Age category totals	18	28	32	22	13	113
Mean education level	3.8	3.7	3.5	3.4	3.8	3.6

[a] The numbers in the body of the table are raw numbers of women except for the bottom row, which reports average scores on a 1 to 5 scale; 12 of 125 respondents did not report their age, and so are not listed in this table.

Figure 3.5 Interviewees' occupations (n = 113), by sector.

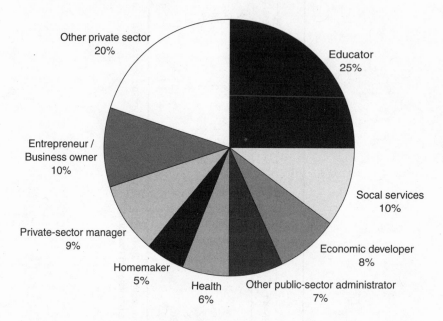

ing that the overall proportion of public sector jobs in the Maritimes was 28.5 per cent at this time (Beaudin 1998, 46).

Among the occupational categories shown in figure 3.5, at 25 per cent the education sector employed the largest number of the women interviewed (28 of the 113 respondents). The majority of them (18) are schoolteachers, while the rest are postsecondary instructors and administrators. Even given the overrepresentation of the public sector, the number of educators is high. Beaudin's results show that roughly one-quarter of public sector jobs are in education, whereas nearly half of the public sector workers interviewed here are educators. It is possible that education comprises a larger proportion of the public sector in rural areas. However, far fewer interviewees work in the health care sector (7, of whom 5 are registered nurses), even though that sector employs a proportion of women similar to that in the education field, in the overall population in the Atlantic ridings where research was conducted, and elsewhere in Canada (Statistics Canada, 1996). It is evident that educators are overrepresented among rural women leaders; this phenomenon is examined more closely in chapter 6.

The social service sector is also well represented, with eleven women reporting occupations such as social worker or counsellor. The strength of this sector lies, in part, with organizations engaged in labour force development. Women providing services contracted by on community economic development projects, for a women's shelter or as career counsellors fall into this category.

Nine women are professionally employed in the economic development field. As will be shown later in the book, this is of particular importance because these women proved to be especially astute observers of, as well as significant players in, the local political scene. Economic developers typically work for economic development boards that are created and regulated by provincial governments as regional-level adjuncts to municipal governments. The operating budgets for these boards, including the salaries for professional staff, are typically cobbled together from all three levels of government. There is no recognized degree that leads to the professional designation of economic developer, and people with a wide variety of education backgrounds are so employed. Membership in the Economic Developers Association of Canada (EDAC) confers the professional designation of Ec.D. This national organization had 508 members in 2001, including nine women interviewed here. Being an economic developer is almost exclusively a rural occupation; urban centres typically employ professional economists with doctorates in economics. The EDAC reports close working ties with Agriculture Canada and the Rural Secretariat of Canada. It seeks to include even the smallest rural economic development boards by offering membership at sharp discounts to people administering annual operating budgets of less than $50,000.

While most participants reported occupations in the public sector, a substantial number work in the private sector, and eleven own and operate their own small businesses. Most of the entrepreneurs brought up the role their business has in the local economy; some gave me their business cards. Additional information about these businesses was obtainable from independent sources, for example, by looking at a website, driving past the place of business, or noting membership in the Chamber of Commerce. It is evident that several of these entrepreneurs are quite wealthy.

Perhaps just as worthy of mention as the details of the participants' occupations is the fact that so many of these women hold jobs at all, in view of the devastatingly high unemployment levels in their communities. The Atlantic provinces have lower employment rates than the rest of Canada, and their rural areas and small towns have the lowest employment rates in the region (Bollman 2000, 2001, 2003). Among the overall adult populations, both men and women, in the federal electoral districts where interviews were conducted, employment rates from the 1996 Census ranged from a low of 33 per cent in Bonavista-Trinity-Conception to a high of 53 per cent in New Brunswick Southwest, and unemployment rates ranged from 14 per cent to 35 per cent (Statistics Canada, 1996). In many of these communities, just having a steady well-paying job is remarkable, especially for middle-aged women. The employment situation of the participants in this study was much more favourable. Among the 124 women who answered the employment status question, twenty-two are retired, eighty are employed, and six are unemployed, while the remaining sixteen are not seeking paid employment (e.g., because they are full-time volunteers or students). These numbers imply a labour force participation rate among the interviewees of approximately 70 per cent, with an employment rate of 65 per cent and an unemployment rate of approximately 7 per cent.

The husbands of the married interviewees are also well employed. All eighty-seven married respondents answered the question on husband's employment status, and not one was listed as unemployed. About a quarter of the husbands worked in the public sector, which is more or less in line with the overall population, whereas their wives were far more likely to be in the public sector. The other husbands represented a wide range of occupations, for example, farmer, aerospace engineer, fisher, entrepreneur, and labourer.

Having paid employment does not get in the way of civic engagement for the participants in this study. Even if we consider only those participants who work as full-time employees, the volunteer level is scarcely affected: 70 per cent of them volunteer for one or more organizations (as compared with 75 per cent overall), and 53 per cent volunteer for several (as compared with 57 per cent). Moreover, the full-time employed same subgroup has the same rate (58 per cent) of working on election campaigns as the overall group, and the highest level of board appointments (47 per cent) among the employment-status subgroups, compared with the overall rate of 38 per cent. Clearly, these women's jobs do not inhibit their civic involvement, and indeed they appear to be a help for activities in which public esteem matters, such as board appointments. A picture emerges of highly active and industrious women who apply their abundant energies in a variety of venues beyond the household.

This picture is consistent with the resource theory of political participation, which holds that socioeconomic status, including employment, propels people into leadership roles. The type of job is important, in part because the skills associated with high-level jobs, for example, chairing meetings and making presentations, are directly transferrable as civic skills. But perhaps even more important than the skills are the social networks that go along with the job. Typically, people do not volunteer independently to serve on the board of an organization. The most effective way to recruit board members is to ask them to serve directly to their faces, and few people refuse when asked directly. When recruiters survey the pool of potential recruits, they see the people who are most visible, often because they hold high-level jobs that are in the public eye. In this way, small differences in career paths add up to larger differences in terms of who becomes a leader (see Burns et al. 2001, chapt. 8; Verba et al. 1995).

Self-appraisal of Leadership Abilities

Interviewees were asked to rate their own leadership potential through a series of questions taken from a U.S. candidate recruitment study. First, generalized personal traits were probed using eight statements with which the respondent was asked to agree or disagree. The responses are summarized in table 3.2. On the whole, these women feel confident in their abilities and accomplishments. Their near unanimity in assuming responsibility is hardly surprising, as this trait closely matches the selection criteria for this study. A large majority of respondents (84 per cent) reported frequently giving advice to others. The notation '(emp)' is added to this entry in table 3.2 to indicate that employment status has a significant association with this trait.[7] Only 50 per cent of respondents not in the workforce (and not retired) identified this trait in themselves, while 100 per cent of the self-employed respondents did so. This same pattern with respect to employment status arose for the question about taking the lead in group activities, that is, self-employed women are very likely (95 per cent) to identify themselves with this trait, while those not in the workforce are far less likely (33 per cent) to do so.[8] Interviewees reported significant differences in their perception of themselves having these traits that varied according to their employment status, which is interesting, considering that they were selected for this study on the basis of others' perception of them having these same traits. Even though it seems reasonable for this relationship to exist in the general population, one might have expected it to have been eliminated in this study by the selection process. The crucial distinction lies in differing perceptions of

Table 3.2 Interviewees' self-rated leadership qualities

	No. of responses	% of respondents who agree with statement
I like to assume responsibility.	123	(96)
I often give others advice and suggestions.	119	(84) (emp)[a]
I usually count on being successful at everything I do.	119	(81) (emp)
I like to take the lead when a group does things together.	121	(70) (emp)
I am good at getting what I want.	115	(67)
I enjoy convincing others of my opinions.	119	(62)
I am often a step ahead of others.	115	(59)
I often notice that I serve as a model for others.	114	(58) (age)[b]

[a] (emp) indicates that employment status has a significant association with respondents' agreement with this statement.
[b] (age) indicates that age has a significant association with respondents' agreement with this statement.

these traits, that is, self-perception versus the perception of the local facilitator who invited them for the study in the first place. Responses to the statement about being successful in most endeavours also displayed a significant dependence on employment status: full-time employees are far more likely to ascribe this trait to themselves, while retirees and those not in the workforce are less likely to do so.[9] These employment-related differences in self-assessment follow job responsibilities, with self-employed women thinking they are especially good at giving advice and taking the lead, and full-time employees thinking they are especially good at doing things.

Given the high grades that interviewees gave themselves in specific leadership traits, it is striking that only a small majority (58 per cent) felt that others see them as role models, despite their qualifications. Only those in the 35 to 44 age group reported strong agreement (88 per cent) with the statement 'I often notice that I serve as a model for others.'[10] But for that one exception, all age, employment, and education categories reported modest results in this regard, which is even more striking when one recalls how many of these interviewees are educators or hold other high-profile jobs that are commonly associated with someone who is a role model. The three least-chosen traits (at the bottom of table 3.2) all depend on the actions and/or opinions of others, whereas the most-chosen ones (at the top of table 3.2) are more internal individual traits of the women themselves. This distinction might even apply to the gap between 'being successful' (81 per cent) and 'getting what I want' (67 per cent). One can logically be successful, in some sense, while still not getting what one wants, especially if the process is unfair. The mismatch between how these women feel about themselves and how they think other people feel about them could be described as a 'role-model paradox.' It indicates a sense of being under-appreciated.

Five other statements were presented to characterize performance or behaviour in specific situations in which leadership plays a role. The average responses are summarized in table 3.3. The first three statements suggest a nuanced approach to risk. A solid willingness to tackle controversial issues was apparent, but respondents were more cautious when it came to financial matters. The remarkable discrepancy between the bottom two statements in table 3.3 relates closely to the role-model paradox that emerged from table 3.2. For the most part, while interviewees feel that they can make an effective public statement, they are far less certain that people would pay much attention to what they have to say.

Many of the women in this study seem to feel that they exercise their

Table 3.3 Interviewees' self-ascribed leadership performance and/or behaviour (scored on a 0–100 scale)

Statement	No. of responses	Score*
I feel free to speak about controversial political issues with close friends.	124	80
I'm not worried about getting into trouble with authorities (police, school, government) by taking a public stand on a controversial issue.	123	82
I feel comfortable taking risks when facing a risky financial or career decision.	125	57
I speak well enough to make an effective statement in public at a community meeting.	123	87
People would pay attention if I made a public statement at a community meeting.	122	60

* The questionnaire allowed for gradations of agreement; the responses were coded on a conventional evenly spaced scale from 0 to 100. 'Score' represents the average score of the respondents.

leadership in a vacuum, in that others do not adequately appreciate their efforts and qualifications or really look up to them. This was eloquently put by an interviewee in one discussion group recalling her experience in working with the Progressive Conservative Party:

> I really enjoyed politics, getting together with the group, going to [the city], and meeting new people. But I got so upset. It hurt so badly that my friends would put their politics or my politics ahead of what I was doing for them. And in all honesty, I worked as hard as I could. I've seen it and I miss it, but I'm so disillusioned now. I've seen it happen to [other women in the group]. It's a shame actually. In this little group, if you listen to what the people are saying and how disillusioned they are, and so are many women.

Her expression of the disappointment that had led her to leave the party prompted another interviewee to comment, 'We seem to eat our own women alive in this county.'

Motives for Participating

Ultimately, the health and vigour of civil society comes down to the question of what motivates people to engage with each other in voluntary associations and thus to produce social capital or build organizational capacity. This question is a long-standing conundrum at the heart of classical empirical work in political participation (see Verba et al. 1995, 99–105). The voluntary pursuit of collective goals in association with other civic actors who are also free and equal individuals is the defining characteristic of civil society. Substantial moral and social pressure can be brought on individuals to participate; nevertheless, civic activity cannot, by definition, be compelled or coerced by law. In this context, economics-based theories of collective action have argued that the optimal strategy for rational actors seeking to maximize individual utility is to withdraw from collective life in favour of their private pursuits. As rational actors, moreover, it is to their advantage to be free riders, that is, to let everyone else do the work of increasing the stock of social capital while enjoying the associated benefits without incurring the costs of participating. From this point of view, it is paradoxical that despite it being in no individual's self-interest to do so, a fair number of people do participate in civic activities.

Indeed, some people, such as the women interviewed here, participate a good deal. What motivates them to be so engaged in public life? This question was posed to the subset of women who had worked for at least one election campaign, and also to those who within the previous two years had been on an official government board. The questionnaire listed fifteen standard motives for civic engagement (Verba et al. 1995) and asked respondents to assess the importance of each in their own decisions to participate in these two activities. The motivations are general and universal, in that they could apply to a wide variety of activities, in most any location or setting. These motives (Burns et al. 2001, 115) typically distinguish the desire to influence government policy from selective benefits to the individual, and the latter category is often subdivided into civic gratifications, social gratifications, and material benefits. Jobs, career advancement, or help with a personal or family problem are examples of material benefits. Social gratifications include the excitement and enjoyment of working with like-minded people on a common project. Civic gratifications refer to the satisfaction of contributing to the public good or of doing one's duty.

The results are summarized in figure 3.6, using a 0 to 100 scale to indicate the importance of each motive in deciding to work on an election campaign and to accept an appointment on a government board. The motives for the two different activities follow nearly the same pattern, in which respondents overwhelmingly cited the importance of civic gratifications such as making the community a better place to live and of carrying out one's duty as a citizen. To lesser degrees, respondents also reported the importance of influencing government policy and of social gratifications, such as being with people who share their ideals. Very few respondents cited material benefits as important motivations. These results are entirely consistent with Verba et al.'s large-scale surveys of (mostly urban) North American public opinion (1995). Civic gratifications are the dominant way in which people everywhere frame and justify their participation, and this is especially so for women. Jeane Kirkpatrick's designation of this tendency as a 'service vocation' to politics (1974, 143–5) definitely applies to this group of community leaders in rural Atlantic Canada.

Partisanship and Ideology

The questionnaire was not designed to probe in detail the value system of the participants. However, three questions help to indicate how well the study was able to access the diversity of ideological approaches that

Figure 3.6 Interviewees' motives for working on election campaigns ($n = 73$) and serving on appointed boards ($n = 47$), scored on a 0–100 scale.

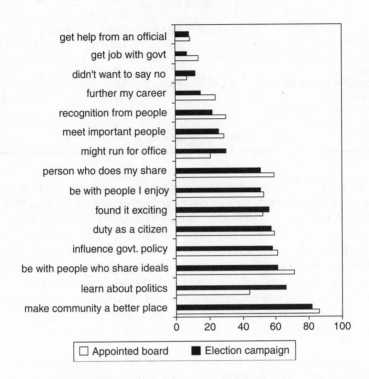

leaders bring to their civic engagement. Two asked about partisan affiliation and membership, while the third was a standard left-right question about the trade-off between social programs and taxes.

Thirty-six of 125 respondents reported being members of a political party: eighteen belong to the Liberal Party, eleven to the PC Party, and six to the NDP.[11] This distribution shows some coverage of the partisan universe, but it applies to only a minority of the interviewees. Partisan affiliation is perhaps a better indicator, as almost everyone answered the question about which party they feel closest to (see far-right column of table 3.4): Thirty-two of these women usually think of themselves as Liberals, thirty-five as Conservatives, and twenty-two as New Democrats; twenty-six explicitly indicated that they are not affiliated with any one party.[12] Some of the latter added notations saying that they prefer to vote for the candidate, based on the issues in a particular election, rather than

Table 3.4 Interviewees' partisan affiliations and left-right orientations

Party affiliation	Taxes/social programs				
	Increase taxes (*n*)	Status quo (*n*)	Cut taxes (*n*)	Reject choice (*n*)	Total
Liberal	8	15	7	2	32
Progressive Conservative	4	20	10	1	35
New Democrat	6	8	5	3	22
Do not favour any one party	4	10	11	1	26
Did not answer	2	4	3	1	10
Total	24	57	36	8	125

for the party. Thus, we have a roughly four-way split among the women associated with the three major political parties in the region and those who reported no party affiliation. While NDP affiliation was not as prevalent as Tory or Liberal, it was higher than overall electoral support for the NDP in these districts in recent years. The New Democrats have been looking for an electoral breakthrough in Atlantic Canada for decades, but sustained electoral success has eluded the party outside of the cities. That NDP support is higher among the interviewees than in the general population suggests that the NDP plays an important role in facilitating women's leadership that goes beyond its electoral showing, even in rural areas.

To get a sense of where interviewees were situated within the left-right ideological spectrum, they were asked to indicate their preferences from among three possibilities: cutting taxes and social programs keeping the status quo, and raising taxes to improve social programs. Almost half (57, or 46 per cent; see bottom row of table 3.4) of the interviewees chose the middle ground, that is, 'keep taxes as they are.' Considering that taxes are relatively high in this region – equivalent to 41 per cent of personal income in Atlantic Canada in 1996, compared with a national average of 37 per cent (McMahon 2000, 35) – it is notable that a significant number of respondents (24, or 19 per cent) favour increased taxes. A somewhat larger minority (36, or 29 per cent) prefer cutting taxes.

Surprisingly, the responses to this left-right question were not strongly associated with party affiliation. As shown in table 3.4, supporters of all three major parties chose the status quo (keeping taxes the same) most frequently. As might be expected, a few more PC supporters chose tax cuts over tax increases, while Liberal and NDP supporters who did not choose the status quo were more evenly split. However, this tendency was not overwhelming, and all positions on this question were represented among the supporters of each political party.

Considering how many women at each meeting were close friends and/or associates, it is astonishing how much variation in partisanship and ideology was found within the groups. At only one meeting – arranged through the Liberal Party – did all interviewees report the same party affiliation. At the two other meetings arranged by a political party there were women who reported affiliation with a different party. NDP affiliation was by no means unanimous at meetings arranged through women's equality organizations; the highest level of NDP affiliation at any one meeting was less than 50 per cent. A meeting arranged through a women's shelter had only one NDP supporter. The meetings with Women's Institute members included NDP supporters, despite this organization's Tory roots. Thus, no strong left-right pattern emerged among the groups. The interviewees reported diverse ranges of partisan affiliation and orientation to familiar left-right issues, and no strong patterns in these responses emerged in relation to age, education, community, and so on – they appear instead to be largely individual choices.

Summary

This chapter showed that the interviewees in this study have active leadership roles in a number of areas, including as candidates for elected office, campaign workers, appointees on official government boards, and as volunteers for a wide range of organizations. Civic gratification was most commonly cited as the primary motive for engaging in these activities. Social gratification was also cited, as was the opportunity to influence policy, but material benefit was cited far less often. These women are exceptionally well educated, as the majority of them have postsecondary degrees, across all age groups. On the whole, they are employed in prominent occupations, most frequently in the public sector. Their self-assessment of their leadership characteristics shows that the interviewees are, for the most part, confident in their own abilities. However, they are significantly less confident in other people's appraisal of them, in terms of their abilities and appreciation for their efforts – a 'role-model paradox.' Responses to the study questionnaire reveal significant diversity in partisanship and ideology among rural women leaders in the region. Taken together, these results show that many of them possess the skills, experience, and socioeconomic and psychological resources that equip individuals to be successful and prominent, and more than a few participants in this study could be included in a pool of credible potential candidates for elected office.

Does a woman in rural Atlantic Canada have to be highly educated, well employed, and married to a well-employed husband before she can play a leadership role in her community? If so, it would mean that the bar has been set very high for women in communities whose economies are decidedly not thriving. The questionnaire responses suggest that what Roberto Michels identified as 'the iron law of oligarchy,' for nine-teenth-century socialist parties of Europe (1962 [1915]), continues to operate across voluntary organizations in rural Atlantic Canada today. A criterion for high socioeconomic status would definitely contribute to limiting the women's leadership pool.

These results go a long way towards understanding who the women interviewed here are. We have learned a good deal about the back-grounds and related experiences of these women who stand out in their communities, and now have a solid basis for interpreting their com-ments in the discussions on local political dynamics that are examined in the following chapters.

4 Images of Leadership

Throughout their careers successful politicians develop, nurture, and protect a public image created expressly for public consumption. This persona is usually an exaggerated and, hopefully, enhanced characterization of the individual's natural strengths that resonates with cultural or national imagery. It thus appeals to voters' self-perception as citizens of their nation and inspires their confidence in a leader. Prime Minister Jean Chrétien's presentation of himself as 'le petit gars de Shawinigan,' for example, resonated with mainstream Liberal Party voters, in spite of all his impressive credentials as a lawyer and businessman. In the United Kingdom during the 1980s, Prime Minister Margaret Thatcher successfully projected an image of the 'Iron Lady' that personified her neo-conservative policy agenda in terms that resonated with Imperial British mythography. The imagery further captured Thatcher's gender as a source of political strength, as opposed to traditional images of feminine weakness and lack of resolve. Janice MacKinnon, the Saskatchewan minister of finance who balanced that province's books in the 1990s, was known as 'Combat Barbie.' But these are exceptionally successful politicians. For most politicians, the task is more difficult. Pat Lorjie, a long-serving Saskatchewan politician, said that developing a public profile is like walking a fine-edged blade; publicity is almost always good, but women, she thought, more so than men, risk becoming caricatures of themselves in a way that demeans and discredits them.[1]

This chapter examines how rural women leaders in Atlantic Canada perceive leadership in the abstract, as a prelude to subsequent chapters that focus on their concrete personal experiences in their communities. It presents their views of what a leader should look like, identifies the women they particularly admire and aspire to emulate, and discusses their perceptions of the experiences of women at high levels of power.

Looking the Part

Part of being a successful politician is looking the part. Even before the advent of mass communications technologies, a politician's public persona was primarily represented as a visual image. But what image should a contemporary middle-aged woman project? Even someone as successful as Manitoba politician Sharon Carstairs – leader of the Manitoba Liberal Party in 1984 and a senator since 1994 – talked of her own ongoing struggle with this question:

> It quickly became apparent that my clothes, the fact that I was quite content to let my hair go grey and the size and shape of my glasses were also subject to active discussion by both the media and the public ... Fifteen years have now passed since I began to question why I was subjected to such physical scrutiny. How much of this was a gender issue? How much of it was just plain stubbornness on my part? Why was I so unwilling to play the game? After all, I could have coloured my hair. I simply refused, and yet there is no question in my mind that a number of male politicians in their fifties and sixties are doing just that. (2000, 313)

To be a female politician is a specific performance of gender. If the Iron Lady was an effective female image during Britain's Falkland War, what analogous image might be effectively employed by ambitious women in Atlantic Canada today? Is there a single public image universal to postindustrial societies; or are there country-specific or rural-urban distinctions, or does an image resonate only with voters in a geographically bound electoral district? Having identified such a public image, is there a conflict between that image and a woman's own perception of herself? Would a potential candidate for office feel comfortable dressing up and performing the 'gender' of a political woman, or would she feel like a fraud? For aspiring politicians, these are very practical questions.

To delve into this issue, a visual device was used as an ice-breaker exercise at the meetings.[2] Four photographs were shown of the same woman, but made up in four different ways (see figure 4.1). Leonie Huddy (1998) designed this device to capture conventional gender stereotypes, and arranged it as follows: Feminine images are on the top, and non-feminine images on the bottom; non-career images are on the left, and career images on the right. According to these conventions, Photograph A would be interpreted as feminine and non-career; Photograph B as feminine and career; and so forth. In our meetings, I did not begin by

Figure 4.1 Gender-stereotype photographs used in image exercises with interviewees (A to D).

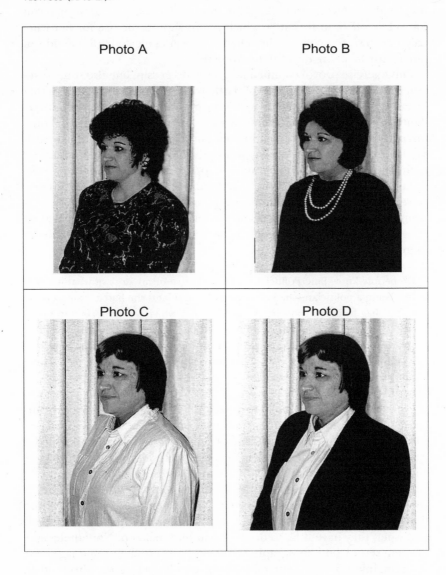

identifying these intended conventions but, rather, asked participants the following three questions: (1) Which photo looks most like you, or do you identify with most? (2) If the woman in these photos were to run for public office in this area, which photo should she use for her campaign posters, to maximize her chances of being elected? (3) Could you pin a party label on any of these women?

This exercise provoked much laughter and gossip, but also some resistance because a good number of participants resented the very idea that image should count at all, as opposed to a candidate's established credentials, record of community service, and personal integrity. Some interviewees refused to recommend a campaign image or to put a partisan label on any image. More typically, they would begin by establishing their personal objection to basing opinion on image, and then, having so distanced themselves, move on to a discussion of how others would perceive the images. For example, one interviewee said that she was 'stunned and appalled' by the meticulous attention given to personal appearance while campaigning but conceded the necessity for it with the following anecdote:

> Do people know Jane Politician?[3] She told me a funny story of what it was like being a politician. She had been to London and she had a really good quality bag from Harrod's [department store], which was important to her because she didn't want it to rip apart, and she carried it everywhere. While she was on the plane, someone said to her 'You are not going to last long as a politician with a bag like that.' So she unstitched the Harrod's logo and put [her provincial] logo on it.

It is interesting that the politician herself felt obliged to justify the purchase in practical terms rather than style or prestige. Despite the widespread distaste for the importance of image, respondents articulated a clear and definite understanding of those perceptions, as a begrudging consensus emerged about each of the three questions.

In response to the question 'which photo looks most like you, or do you identify with most?' interviewees would often joke that most of the time they look like C, but that they aspire to look like A and B on a good day, when they have time to do their hair and makeup. Nonetheless, 41 per cent settled on Photograph B as being closest to their self-image, and the remaining 59 per cent split almost evenly among the three other photographs (see figure 4.2).

Figure 4.2. Interviewees' self-image, self-selected from photos A to D in Figure 4.1.

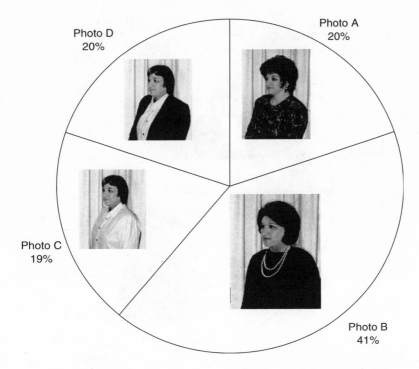

Greater consensus emerged about the recommended campaign photo (see figure 4.3). Fully 66 per cent of respondents recommended that if the woman were to run for public office locally – whatever the type of election – she should use the image in Photograph B for her campaign posters. That B was also the most frequent choice corresponding to respondents' own self-image suggests that quite a few of the interviewees feel confident that their own self-image helps to support their leadership goals. While B was the clear favourite, one seasoned campaigner pointed out that there is no one correct answer. She described her own campaign practice of changing outfits to accommodate cultural expectations that varied from one polling area to another and to make practical accommodations for climbing up and down boat ladders when visiting outport islands.

Figure 4.3 Interviewees' preferred election campaign image, self-selected from photos A to D in Figure 4.1.

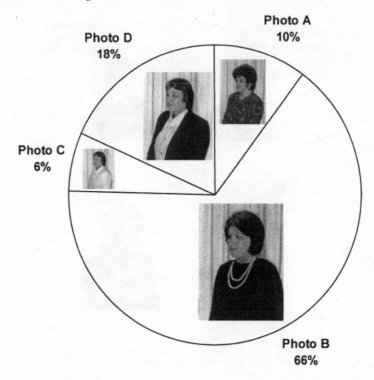

I was left wondering what this woman meant by 'cultural expectations,' until she returned to this point in response to the 'Harrod's bag' story:

> I'm going to break it down to a francophone/anglophone issue in rural New Brunswick. That Harrod's handbag would be quite acceptable if you were a politician from the north because they expect that. They expect politicians – male and female – to maintain this [image], to have the sports car and vrrrroom. If it was a male, not one of his constituents would question it, but I can tell you, you wouldn't find him campaigning in [anglophone] county with the wind whipping through his hair. It just wouldn't be, but it is acceptable in the north.

Others in the group agreed that 'the more flamboyant, the better' in

Figure 4.4 Interviewees' association of image with political party, selected from photos A to D in Figure 4.1.

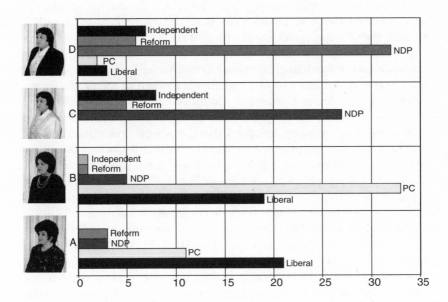

francophone parts of the province. In concrete terms, these considerations led one interviewee to conclude that the more flamboyant '[photo] A would represent francophone New Brunswick and B would represent anglophone New Brunswick.' I had not anticipated a linguistic dimension to these images; however, this same generalization emerged in several groups, in which A was perceived to be the francophone – either Quebec or Acadian – image and B was perceived to be the anglophone image.

Participants pinned party labels or stereotypes to each of the photos (see figure 4.4). The more conventionally feminine A and B images were identified with the two traditionally dominant parties (Liberals and Conservatives), while the less conventionally feminine C and D were identified most frequently with the NDP. There was substantial consensus that photograph B suits Tory women best, while A represents a Liberal candidate. This pattern fits in well with the linguistic stereotype discussed above, as francophone voters have traditionally supported the Liberal Party. In regard to the Reform Party, the most striking result is that so few women in Atlantic Canada have a preconceived idea about what a

Reform woman might look like; there were only fifteen mentions of the Reform Party, most of which were placed with the photos that were perceived as less successful campaign images. Even the Independent category received more mentions than that. A lack of familiarity with a Reform Party image is consistent with that party's lack of visibility in the region. As the Reform Party became the Canadian Alliance Party, which has since merged with the Progressive Conservative Party, at the national level, it is not ever likely to make further inroads into the political consciousness of Atlantic Canadians. Considering the deep roots of the Tories in Atlantic Canada, and the continuity in party membership and leadership that has been sustained there, it seems reasonable to infer that in this region the images associated with the new Conservative Party of Canada would more closely resemble those previously associated with the PC Party than with Reform. Very different transitions have followed the merger of the conservative parties in other regions, and so we would expect the transfer of images to vary accordingly.

How unique to rural Atlantic Canada are the interviewees' perceptions of image? It is not necessary to study a parallel urban group to get a rough answer to this question. Preference for the image in Photograph B as a political leader is deeply entrenched in contemporary western culture. Almost everyone has seen photographs of Eleanor Roosevelt (in the 1950s) and Judy LaMarsh (in the 1960s) wearing the identical uniform – black dress, white pearls, and smoothly coiffed hair. Many female politicians to this day – for example, former federal Liberal cabinet minister Anne McLellan – cultivate more than an accidental resemblance. Out of curiosity about how ubiquitous these image perceptions are, I asked the same three questions about these photos to students in two of my classes. Considering the vast age discrepancy between them and these interviewees, I was surprised to find that the distribution of the students' responses was almost identical to that of the rural women leaders in my study. A clear preference for photograph B emerged, both for self-identification and campaign image. Photograph A was identified with the Liberal Party (with PC as second choice), B with the PC Party (with Liberal as second choice), and both C and D were identified equally and nearly exclusively with the NDP. The only noticeable distinction was a greater disdain among the students for photograph A as representing their self-image. Further independent corroboration emerged regarding linguistic stereotypes when scholars of Quebec and Acadian politics attending my conference presentations confirmed that image A would conform to francophone conventions throughout Canada, in both rural and urban areas. These considerations strongly suggest that the overall perceptions of visual image expressed by the rural women leaders in the present study (summarized in figures 4.2 to 4.4) are based on broad cultural perceptions that are neither uniquely rural nor uniquely Atlantic Canadian.

To be sure, certain nuances did emerge that suggested a rural twist. For example, the degree to which the interviewees felt obliged to premise the discussion with strong objections to the very idea that visual image matters may be a rural characteristic. Certainly, my students did not register any such distaste. In most cases, the women in this study know the candidates in their ridings and communities, as can be said for many other rural voters who are less active politically. Perhaps this leads to a greater expectation that looks should not count for much. As another example, ten different interviewees in several different groups stated – to much murmured agreement – that the woman in photograph B would be better off without the pearls. Their reasoning suggests a rural, although not specifically Atlantic, sensibility. The pearls, it was said, 'were intimidating,' 'would throw people off because they symbolize money,' look 'Ottawa-ish,' look like the 'Queen Mum,' or weren't appropriate for dealing with people in the resource industries of mining, fishery, and forestry. These conversations made it evident that the interviewees regard pearls as powerful symbols of female prestige and authority and that a considerable number of them felt deep anxiety and discomfort about exercising the power that pearls represent.

Role Models

Another key facet in the composite image of leadership involves prototypes to admire and/or emulate. Prominent women play an important role in mobilizing other women to take an interest in public affairs and perhaps later, as a result, to become involved themselves. Nancy Burns et al. compared politics to sports: just as young boys idolize sports heros and learn athletic skills by imitating their heros, and thus grow up to be sports fans, so too, do boys become political fans through a process of admiration and imitation. But whom are young girls to admire? Research by the Burns group found that women pay more attention to politics when other women are featured in media reports and that their political knowledge about an issue or an election is greater when it involves other women. The researchers inferred that female audiences identify with the women politicians being featured, helping to make active engagement in

Figure 4.5 Categories of women admired by interviewees in this study.

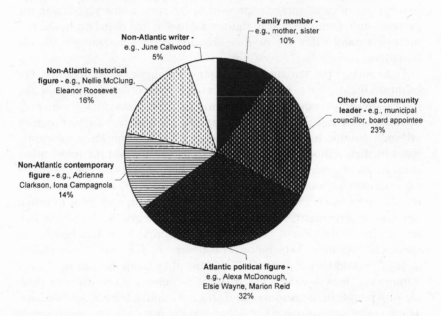

political affairs seem more worthwhile and accessible to them (2001, 341–56). These findings led Burns et al. to propose that building women's leadership in public affairs is a cumulative process, in which each generation of women comes to political maturity with an awareness of the prominent women who preceded them.

The questionnaire in the present study asked each respondent to identify a woman – not necessarily a politician – whom she particularly admired. Responses were extremely varied, and included 111 references to seventy-five different women. Figure 4.5 summarizes these results by putting them into six categories, roughly in order of proximity to the respondent (and likelihood of knowing personally), moving clockwise from the top. The examples listed are the most frequent responses in each category.

The most striking point is just how local the choices are. One-third of the responses involved either family members or other figures in the community.[4] In addition to family members, it is obvious that the respondents know, at least collegially if not personally, local officials, businesswomen, and activists (grouped together in the category of 'local community leader'). In several cases the woman admired was filling out her own questionnaire, just a few chairs down at the same meeting. In one case, a mother and daughter put each other down, and in another case, two friends were each other's 'admirees.' Such mutual admiration is the seed of solidarity and an important building block of successful networks that should, in principle, be an asset during an election campaign.

A further one-third of the women cited are more widely recognized political figures from within Atlantic Canada. All but two are contemporary politicians who within the preceding decade held seats in either the House of Commons or one of the four Atlantic provincial legislatures. This category included the most-cited figures overall, each with seven references: Alexa McDonough, MP for Halifax since 1997 and former leader of the national NDP (1995–2003), and Elsie Wayne, PC MP for Saint John, New Brunswick, from 1993 until her retirement in 2004 (and mayor of Saint John before that). Another oft-cited figure was Marion Reid, who served several terms in the P.E.I. House of Assembly before being appointed lieutenant governor in 1990. The two non-elected exceptions in this category were Anne Derrick, a prominent human-rights litigator, and Muriel Duckworth, a well-known peace activist; both of them are based in Halifax. While few of these admired women actually reside in the communities in which they were cited, it remains very likely that they had had some sort of personal contact with the respondent. These well-known political women travel widely and attend events in various communities that are organized and attended by people like (and including) the interviewees in this study. The proposition that the women cited had had contact with the respondents is further supported by the fact that, even within this group of prominent women, there was a marked preference for proximity. Fourteen of the fifteen admired women in this category were chosen only by respondents who reside in the same province. For example, only women in Prince Edward Island cited Marion Reid or Catherine Callbeck (premier of Prince Edward Island from 1993 until 1996, after which she was appointed to the Senate) or Leone Bagnall (member of P.E.I. House of Assembly from 1979 until 1990). Only women in Nova Scotia mentioned Alexa McDonough. The only exception to this pattern was Elsie Wayne, who was cited by some women in Nova Scotia as well as some in her home province of New Brunswick. This suggests that respondents have a proprietorial attitude towards their role models, much as if they are members of their family or community. Combining the three categories conceptually, we see that nearly two-thirds of the responses involved admired women who were chosen on the basis of proximity.

The remaining one-third of mentions were widely recognized women who were unlikely to have met these respondents. The women from outside Atlantic Canada are grouped (in figure 4.5) into three categories: contemporary public figures, historical public figures, and writers. Among contemporary figures, there was a partisan angle, as some respondents named politicians from within their own parties. For example, only Liberals named Iona Campagnola. One wonders how women in rural Newfoundland would know anything about the lieutenant governor of British Columbia – an appointed position that receives minimal national media coverage. It may be inferred that they know her through her former position as president of the Liberal Party of Canada. Her mention speaks, I think, to the strength of the party and the Liberal Women's Commission, in particular, which sponsored speaking tours and national conventions at which Campagnola appeared. Several New Democrats indicated a strong sense of their party's history in citing Rosemary Brown (who challenged Ed Broadbent for the party's leadership in 1975) or Shirley Douglas (daughter of CCF leader Tommy Douglas and a long-time health-care activist). Other mentioned admirees, such as Hillary Clinton, are internationally well known.

The most frequently cited historical figures were Nellie McClung and Emily Murphy, both early twentieth-century suffragists in western Canada. They were followed by Eleanor Roosevelt, well-known First Lady of the United States during the Depression and Second World War, who later gained renown for her international humanitarian work. The nearly complete absence of responses citing historical figures from Atlantic Canada is sharply at odds with the tendency to admire contemporary local figures or those from the recent past. For example, there was no mention of suffragists Edith Archibald[5] or Armine Gosling.[6] This suggests that the struggle for suffrage in Nova Scotia or Newfoundland, while recognized as important at the time, was never integrated into the collective historical memory of the Atlantic provinces, as it was in the west. Nor was there mention of the first Atlantic Canadian women to attain positions of political power, for example, Gladys Porter,[7] the first woman elected to the Nova Scotia Legislative Assembly; or Muriel McQueen Fergusson,[8] first female speaker of the Senate; or Helena Squires,[9] the first woman elected to the Newfoundland House of Assembly. Why were the achievements of these, and other notable women not seized upon as collective markers of progress?

Finally, it bears remarking that nearly all of the admired women were cited for some sort of political role. As already noted, most of the respondents cited elected or appointed officials at some level of government, even though the question specified that the choice need not be a politician. Respondents who named their own mother or mother-in-law usually chose them for their record of public service in the community, rather than for their role within the family. Only in one case did a respondent cite a relative for overcoming her personal difficulties. While some of the cited international celebrities, such as Lady Diana and Mother Teresa, are not generally recognized as conventionally political figures, they are nonetheless admired for their service to humanity.

Cautionary Tales of Powerful Women

If a political leader is particularly admired by the rural women community leaders in this study, it surely matters what has happened to that woman in the public eye and how the interviewees perceive this. While group discussions were focused primarily on the local community, several touched on prominent women leaders in the national or provincial legislatures. In every instance, these discussions centred on stories of negative experiences endured by the protagonist – cautionary tales of women's humiliation and failure in public life, serving to warn women off the pursuit of power.

A well-known case in point involves Kim Campbell's brief leadership of the Progressive Conservative Party, during which she served as prime minister of Canada prior to the party's disastrous defeat in the 1993 national election. Respondents described Campbell as having been 'set up from the beginning to be the fall guy' for the party on its way down. That she achieved what no other Canadian woman had before, or since, was not mentioned at all. Neither was the fact that she bounced back on her feet with a plum diplomatic appointment as Canada's consul-general in Los Angeles, which was followed by a prestigious chair at Harvard University.

Another cautionary tale featured Jane Stewart's experience in the spring of 2000 when, as minister responsible for Human Resources and Development Canada in Jean Chrétien's Liberal government, she came under severe criticism for financial mismanagement – dating back to incidents that had occurred long before her tenure. Stewart appeared regularly on television, as she defended her department against the Reform Party Opposition MPs during question period and against reporters during media scrums. It is a textbook truism that such is the routine duty of cabinet ministers in the Westminster model of government. Chrétien and his caucus agreed that Stewart had acquitted herself admirably in the difficult circumstances. She thus secured the appreciation of her colleagues, and thereby established herself as a cabinet insider.

Participants in this study perceived the matter differently. They saw Stewart as a woman deliberately set up by her own male colleagues, rather than as someone who manoeuvred deftly through the routine rough-and-tumble of question period and press scrums, with her male colleagues' support. Through the lens of the nightly news camera, participants had seen close-up views of Stewart standing up in the House of Commons; they did not see her being backed up by the Liberal Party team. Ironically, the Opposition attack on this issue was led by another woman – Reform MP Diane Ablonczy – who might equally have been remembered as the central character of this story, but was not. The attacks on Stewart seemed to strike a raw nerve among the rural women interviewed, perhaps because it spoke directly to their own fears about the consequences of acquiring power.

Even Elsie Wayne was the subject of a cautionary tale, even though she had enjoyed nearly uninterrupted electoral success at both the municipal and federal levels. The topic and dynamic of the discussion about Wayne is both amusing and instructive:

SPEAKER 1: [Elsie Wayne] has been really publicized lately.

SPEAKER 2: That was not fair, not fair whatsoever.

SPEAKER 1: According to the newspaper she was the most poorly dressed MP, which I can't agree with. For a woman her size, I think she carries herself very well.

SPEAKER 3: The store that sells her her clothing was very put out. They said she dresses very classical.

SPEAKER 1: It suits her, for her figure and for her age.

SPEAKER 4: It was probably some young punk writing the article.

Despite their near unanimous rejection of the importance of physical appearance, the interviewees cared a great deal about what was being said about the appearance of Elsie Wayne, and they had evidently discussed it together prior to the meeting. Speaker 2 knew exactly what Speaker 1 was getting at before she said it, and the others cued in immediately, as well. All four interviewees were familiar with and concerned about this (arguably minor) issue. If Wayne, whom they admire and wish to emulate, had such a rough ride, how could they themselves not but fail? But Wayne did not fail, not in the least. She was a successful politician who dressed to appeal to the voters of New Brunswick, not to Ottawa journalists, and judging from the comments cited above, she knew just how to do it.

The interviewees' comments convey a keen sensitivity to media scrutiny of women at the national level. This may be partly because media coverage is more aggressive than these women are used to in their own communities. One group discussion featured the editor of a local newspaper who spoke directly about her responsibilities as a journalist:

> Speaking as a member of the media, we don't get into the mudslinging contests that you would have [in the city]. I knew two of the three provincial candidates running in the last election. As a reporter, I knew where they're from, and it's not an issue of digging up mud in a rural newspaper or rural radio station. It's more presenting the facts and letting people make a choice. It is not that [urban] media 'go for the jugular' attitude from the press. It is not the same political race because people know each other more ... My favourite catch phrase to tell new reporters coming from journalism school is: 'You don't crap on your own doorstep.' Because you can write a scathing editorial, say, that the mayor is an s.o.b., but you'll run into him in [grocery store] tomorrow and you'll have to 'duck and cover.' I've worked in a big city as a journalist and it's totally different. You have almost total anonymity [as a journalist], so you can go for the jugular, or go to a meeting and be an absolute pain in the butt, because you're not going to see these people, chances are, ever again unless you end up in a courtroom being sued by them. So it's a totally different atmosphere.

These comments correspond closely to David Rayside's analysis of small-town Ontario where he said: 'The room for press manoeuvre in criticizing established institutions or dominant ideas is even narrower in small communities, where the need to avoid controversy that "makes the town look bad" imposes severe limits on what a reporter or editor can write' (1991, 250). Lack of critical media coverage in rural communities may well correspond to the absence of critical debate in local politics, which speaks poorly for the quality of democracy. That said, it would not be expected to deter the electoral ambitions of women who are sensitive to public scrutiny and criticism.

Not all of the cautionary tales told in the interviews involved the mass media spotlight. Others involved local consequences of acquiring power. In one discussion group, three women recalled the vicious gossip and sexualized slander that circulated during the career of a prominent provincial politician:

SPEAKER 1: Take the situation of Jane Politician. When Jane went to cabinet, look at all the stories that went around about her; they were absolutely disgusting.

SPEAKER 2: They said that she was just a bitch. The big story was how many secretaries she went through, that there was a new secretary every month because she was such a horrible person – which is the furthest from the truth.

SPEAKER 3: It is [wrong] because my friend was her secretary for years.

SPEAKER 1: Then there were all these crude jokes that Jane was sleeping with the premier: 'Well, she had to be to get into cabinet.' It was just awful. It must have been terrible for her and her family because of the stories going around.

It should be mentioned that these rumours never entered the public sphere, and they never affected the career of this politician. Nevertheless this gossip was remembered and repeated for years after. Speakers 1 and 2 are intimately familiar with political life, and they know exactly what lies in store for any politician. Yet they recounted this cautionary tale for the consumption of two university students sitting at the table, both wide-eyed with curiousity.

A different tale of local consequences involves Claudette Bradshaw, an important figure inside the Chrétien government who, at the time of the interviews, was minister of labour as well as the regional minister for New Brunswick. In spite of the power and prestige of Bradshaw's office, it was the hostile circumstances of her original nomination in 1997 that were remembered by one of the interviewees:

> Claudette did well because she was not the one that the [Liberal] Party wanted. When she ran for nomination, there were four people in Moncton that joined the party, got the ticket and got her elected. The party itself had another name that they wished to have elected. It was a split convention and people left after she won. That's why she had to do quite a bit of repair work. She and her people worked hard out on the street.

This story is not simply an example of fear-mongering. The speaker's tone of admiration made it clear that she recognized the value of the conflict and subsequent reconciliation. Indeed, a fiercely fought and won nomination carries greater weight in caucus than does an uncontested nomination bestowed from above. While this tale may help inhibit

women's ambitions, it also conveys a rational appreciation for how difficult it is to acquire such a high level of power.

On reflection, there is little basis for caution in any of the tales told during the discussions in this study. Each one, even that of Kim Campbell,
could equally be told as a success story involving great achievement in the
face of adversity. Why then would the conventional script for talking
about political ambition turn on a cautionary tale about the powerful
woman brought down low? This pattern prompts the question of whether
their personal experiences of public life in their own communities have
predisposed them to this collectively held image. Thus, we now turn to
the interviewees' own experiences.

Summary

This chapter asked about subjective perceptions of leadership – what
women leaders look like, which women come to mind as admired figures, and what lessons are to be taken from the experiences of prominent women leaders. Most participants expressed disapproval of the
emphasis on physical appearance of politicians and a reluctance to
choose from among the representative photographs that they were
shown. Nevertheless, when pressed, participants had definite preferences for how to dress as a professional politician, and most said they
would feel comfortable dressing up and presenting themselves in public
as that sort of woman. They also expressed strong ideas about which
images correspond to which Canadian political parties. It was shown that
their perceived dress code is entirely consistent with dominant urban
conventions throughout the western world. Only minor rural nuances in
perceptions of visual image were found.

The women chosen as role models were extremely varied, but most
respondents showed a preference for proximity and a bias towards public
service. In large part, the interviewees admired women from within the
same province whose personal style in terms of appearance, demeanour,
and speech, is within reach of being emulated. One-third of the admired
women are either family members or other local community leaders. A
further one-third are women prominent in Atlantic Canada, almost all of
them chosen by interviewees in the same province, suggesting a proprietorial attitude towards role models – much as if they were honorary members of the community or family. Thus, two-thirds of the responses
involved admired women chosen on the basis of proximity. The remain-

ing one-third of the women mentioned are from outside Atlantic Canada: they are either contemporary public figures, historical public figures, or writers. Almost no historical figures from Atlantic Canada were mentioned, suggesting that the struggle for suffrage, and other political advances by women, were never fully integrated into the collective historical memory of the Atlantic provinces, as it was in western Canada.

Several discussions touched on the experiences of prominent women in the national or provincial legislatures – Kim Campbell, Jane Stewart, Elsie Wayne, and Claudette Bradshaw. While these discussions involved stories that differed in detail, all of them followed a common script of a cautionary tale of women's humiliation and failure in public life. Some of the comments of the interviewees convey a keen sensitivity to public scrutiny in the mass media. Others conveyed concern for the local consequences of acquiring power and a fear of conflict with their friends and neighbours – and their families, as we shall see in the following chapter.

5 The Slushy Intersection between Politics and Family

Atlantic Canada is reputed to be distinguished by a particularly strong sense of family. While most everyone claims family closeness as a distinctive cultural characteristic, there are solid grounds for making this claim about Atlantic Canada. The majority of people, particularly in rural areas, are descended from immigrants who arrived in a series of waves from the seventeenth to the mid-nineteenth century. Since then large-scale immigration has ceased, and as a result the basic social structure of the region remains nearly as formed almost two centuries ago, more closely resembling that of Europe than any other part of North America (Conrad and Hiller 2001). This long-term stability is especially marked in rural communities because the relatively few newcomers that do arrive in the region prefer to settle in urban centres. Under these circumstances, it is entirely plausible that a premium on family closeness reproduces itself in a sort of positive-feedback loop. It is a near tautology that people who have returned to their home towns, and those who have never left, are more likely to have close extended-family ties than those who have moved away permanently.

Interviewees in this project described an environment of pervasive intimacy, in which family relationships intersect and spill over into every walk of life, including politics. This chapter examines their perceptions of the interaction between family life and their own civic involvement. Women of all ages articulated this theme most strongly in terms of being able to spend a great deal of time with children or grandchildren, as well as a broad preference for a life centred on a cycle of events and celebrations among a network of extended-family relations. These expectations obviously introduce the potential for gender-role constraints on how much time many women have available for leadership activities outside the family, especially considering the particularly onerous responsibili-

ties of a rural politician. The first section of this chapter reports interviewees' perceptions of the job of a rural politician and to what extent
they themselves have been deterred by the conflict with their family
responsibilities. But gender-role constraints are only one component of
the intersection between family and public life. The second section of
this chapter illustrates how participants conceptualize their families as a
sort of corporate unit, in the sense that the individuals' successes and
failures are shared by, and reflect on, all members. The next two sections
examine two conventional stereotypes of politics in rural Atlantic Canada that are associated with the model of a family as such a corporate
unit: the family vote and family legacies of power and influence. Most
often the interviewees brought up stereotypes as a convenient script
familiar to everyone at the table, which led to a more nuanced and true-
to-life account of public life as they know it.

Gender-role Constraints: Family Responsibilities versus the Job of a Rural Politician

The time and energy that political engagement takes away from one's
family life was a common theme in the discussions with these rural
women leaders. This topic usually came up near the beginning of meetings, when nervous participants began with the 'safe' topic of confirming
the conventional premium on family closeness. To appreciate the potential for this conflict to act as a barrier to electoral ambitions, it is important to understand how participants perceive the job of being a rural
politician. They made it clear that the role of a rural politician is prohib-
itively onerous. Consider the following discussion led off by an economic
development officer:

> The realities of [a politician's job] are frightening – the silly phone calls at
> night, the constant phone calls. This is awful, but [counting on her fingers]
> I didn't get this cheque, or this bill needs to be paid, or I want this pothole
> fixed, or a whole series of things – phone calls like that would disrupt my life
> plenty. And they are still not satisfied with anything in the end.

When I suggested that the constituency office must handle such minor
queries, there was much laughter at my naïveté, and the economic development officer continued:

> We feel that we own our politicians. That means own them twenty-four
> hours a day. Not me personally, but the public at large, that it gives them

the right to call them at whatever time of day or night that they feel appropriate. It also gives them the right to approach you, at whatever time of day or night, in a different light at the grocery store. There is no differentiation between your personal and professional life.

Another woman said that even being on the local executive of the Canadian Legion made it impossible for her to do her business in town without being accosted by people. As a result, she regularly drove more than an hour to do her shopping in a larger urban centre. For this she was scolded by a school board official who said that the best campaigning happens while doing grocery shopping.

At another meeting a woman who had recently run, unsuccessfully, as a candidate in a provincial election voiced a similar understanding:

It would be nothing to pick up the telephone and call your municipal, provincial, or federal representative in this province on your issue. You're calling because the road wasn't sanded properly, or you haven't had adequate number of weeks of work; all of those issues.

Astonishingly, this same participant went on to claim that the demands overflow beyond the elected member:

John Politician is the elected member in this area. I ran against John in the last provincial election and I get thirty-five, forty calls a week. And it doesn't matter that I'm not the elected representative. John Politician is the elected representative. Because you ask people, 'Why are you calling me?' 'Well [they say] I know how it works, [your party's] government is in, and I want this done.'

The group then reached a consensus that it is important for politicians to handle constituents' concerns personally, as opposed to delegating them to staff in the constituency office.

Several straightforward rural – urban distinctions illustrate why rural politicians might have particularly onerous obligations to their constituents.[1] The work of representation is undeniably made more difficult because rural electoral districts are geographically larger than urban districts and thus require more travel. It may also be more difficult because of disparities in 'system-manipulation skills' between rural and urban voters. The greater proportion of urban voters with formal education means that more constituents can be counted on to have a sense of how government bureaucracies are organized; they are more likely to phone the relevant government office themselves than ask their elected member to phone on their behalf. Or in the case of a dispute, urban voters might be more likely to hire themselves a lawyer rather than depend on local politicians to defend them. A third major distinction is the proportionately greater role of the public sector in the local economy; this effect will be explored in some detail in subsequent chapters.

Some women cited the time factor as a barrier to women running for office, insofar as it conflicts with traditional gender roles and family responsibilities. For example, the defeated candidate referred to above explained:

> I'm single, so all I have is 'me, myself and I.' If I had family responsibilities, I'm not sure I could take forty calls a week in a job that is not mine. You know the job is *John's*. My job is [another job] and then I have my volunteer work, so that makes it possible. A big issue in this riding is that women don't have the time. But that's life in rural [part of province]. The challenges are there, but if you have a family plus a full-time job, you know, it's not an option that a lot of women would have the time to commit to.

Interestingly, interviewees invariably attributed this deterrent to other women in the hypothetical abstract (as above), but not directly to themselves. The only concrete example from the interviews of family responsibilities directly limiting political ambitions involved the ambitions of a man, not a woman:

> My husband has been eighteen years in municipal politics. It's become a way of life for us, and we've been able to separate our family life from politics. He did have some aspirations to go provincial, but I knocked down that idea because I didn't want to raise five children on my own. We managed to do everything with our children as others do. Sometimes I did [child-centred activities] alone, but we did a good job ... My husband and I go in two different directions. My husband goes into politics and I'm more into community development and organizations. Politics is not my interest. I support him and help him, but it is just not my thing. He's going to be elected again for sure. That's the kind of marriage we have. We support one another.

The woman speaking was no slouch herself in public affairs. She was a long-standing pillar of the Women's Institutes, serving at the district and provincial level in one capacity or another for many years. Thus, it could be inferred that her veto of her husband's higher ambitions translated into her greater participation in public affairs at the expense of her husband's career. This example drives home the point that the traditional gender roles of husband and father also conflict with the demands of elected office. Not many men have the option or inclination to commit substantial amounts of time to politics, and most women do not, either.

But the interviews did not involve 'most women.' The study's selection process brought to the table a subset of women who are especially active in public affairs. This could go a long way to explaining the relative dearth of complaints about family responsibilities preventing them from taking on public responsibilities. More typically the participants in this study described accommodations that they had struck with their husbands and families.

> I always enjoyed politics. Several parties came after me through the years, but I never gave it much consideration because my husband always told me if I got involved in politics he would divorce me. And he was serious. So I had to decide not to run. I mean I'm quite content in this marriage, so why would I jeopardize it? So finally when I did seek the nomination [for a provincial seat], I said, 'You know it's too bad that women don't have support from their husbands. I think it's a deterrent against running.' I brought that up several times, and one night he looked at me and said, 'For the love of Jesus, run.' And I said, 'You're ready for a divorce are you?' and he said, 'No, I didn't say that.' So I took that as a 'Yes' [that I could run].

This woman went on to win the nomination and the seat and was subsequently appointed to cabinet. Her husband carried through on his promise not to stand in the way, but not to help, either. He did no campaigning and attended no social events, although he did take phone messages. She was grateful that he was at home waiting for her late at night, and not, as she put it, out drinking to 'pay up' for her absence. In fact, she went on to describe how her husband's recalcitrance had inadvertently helped her to be a more accessible politician:

> My motivation for running was the fact that we don't have a lot of rural people elected, whether male or female. Because what is the one thing politicians do when they get elected? They take the wife and kids and go to [provincial capital], and it is so much easier on a Friday afternoon when you're tired, to say, 'I'm not going out in the District; I am going to put my feet up and relax for the weekend because no one is following me.' But because my family was out in the district, I came out every single weekend.

On Sunday morning, I would sit down with a cup of tea and a newspaper, and I would say 75 per cent of these Sunday mornings the phone was ringing or people were walking in; they'd catch me in my robe with a cup of tea. And your home is an open door. But I ran because I believe we do need more rural people in the [legislature]. If you are just coming out [to the district less often] you don't have the same handle on everything that you would if your family was out here keeping you informed and you're coming yourself.

She also saw direct benefits to her policymaking efforts as a cabinet minister:

I had more of an affinity to the people or the clients that I was representing in that department because if I go to a wedding in [a town in her district], I am in the same circle of people that are clients of the department. I go to the post office; they are there. I taught their kids, so I know who these people are. You can sort out in your mind what is good and what is bad for these people, and how it is going to affect them. If I were living in [the capital city], chances are, my circle of friends would never involve these people, and I would not be able to put a face to any [policy decision] that happened.

The excerpts above present a vivid illustration of how the nature of rural representation and gender-role constraints converged in one woman's personal experience as a rural politician. In her case, balancing the conflicts so often cited as deterrents to women's political ambitions – reluctant husband, distance to legislature, and the responsibilities of a rural politician – produced a powerful synergy that she took pride in. This woman was far from typical in her success as a politician, and she was admired for that success. But she was also admired for her attitude towards family conflicts, and many if not most of the interviewees shared her approach to gender-role constraints. As an example, in response to the bathrobe incident, a municipal politician in the same group agreed emphatically, and with evident pride, that her life too was an 'open book' and that her door was always open.

Along these lines, several other groups seemed to feature a certain competitiveness regarding willingness and ability to cope with time demands. In one group, a town councillor and school board trustee (who had never spoken to each other before) found common ground in being able to call regularly upon their husband's parents to collect their children from school and feed them, while they attended political meetings in the evenings. Both made a point of dismissing the threat of divorce because there was such general pressure from in-laws and from the church community to stay married and work through bad times. One woman even claimed that her activities outside the home made her more attractive to her husband; in her eyes, holding elected office brought a whirl of intrigue, passion, and sociability to the marriage that her husband would not be able to match with another woman. In another group, a woman spoke with pride about how she had run for Mi'kmaq band council, both successfully and unsuccessfully, despite having five children to care for at home. She wondered why other women felt constrained by gender roles and asked the rhetorical question: 'Are we, as women, using the guilt thing, the mothering thing as an excuse for our fear of losing?'

The obligations of a rural politician to constituents are clearly onerous, as are the family responsibilities of being a wife and mother. Is the conflict between the two a major barrier to qualified women? It is important to keep in mind that the participants in this project are active and energetic in community affairs, whether or not their activities are directed towards elected office. These are women who, for the most part, make it clear that they have gone out of their way to seek additional responsibilities outside the home. In retrospect, having heard their comments, we can see that it would be out of character for most of them to claim to be deterred from elected office by the mere existence of time intrusion and responsibilities. Overall, the time intrusion per se of a rural politician's responsibilities did not emerge as a dominant barrier to running for elected office among the majority of the women interviewed here. It is very possible that family responsibilities act as a barrier for other women, who were not interviewed for this project, as they are for some men (albeit perhaps to a lesser degree). But not meeting the selection criteria for this project means that a woman is not participating in public life in a significant manner. Thus, the most that can be said for gender-role constraints is that they may limit the numbers of women entering the lowest levels of participation in public life. We have found little, if any, evidence that gender-role constraints introduce a cap on a woman's ambitions in rural Atlantic Canada, once she is in the loop. (This is not to say there is no cap – different factors that have that effect are discussed in later chapters.) If anything, the interviews showed that, in some cases, being embedded in a network of traditional extended-family ties can facilitate a motivated woman's leadership, in terms of both logistical and emotional support.

The Family as a Corporate Unit

The results of the preceding section do not imply that decisions about participating in public life occur independently of family relations. Gender-role constraints, that is, balancing public participation with the time-consuming responsibilities of being a wife and mother in the family home, are only one element in the rich tapestry of family relationships. The following excerpt from one of the interviews conveys a sense of just how deeply embedded the participants are in their families:

SPEAKER 1: I think you'd have more at stake [than an urban politician] because you're not just disappointing your neighbours and your friends; you're disappointing your family. If you don't do well, if you get in that political arena and if you come in third in the election and only have fifteen votes, you've disappointed your entire family, not just neighbours and people you know from work.

SPEAKER 2: And you'd be addressed not as [your own name]; you would be addressed as [your father's] daughter. It's no longer your success or failure. It becomes theirs, and they remind you of it every ten minutes.

SPEAKER 1: When your mom goes to auxiliary at church, and they are talking about that crushing defeat you had in the last election, it's her embarrassment too.

Given that the two speakers above were middle-aged women with substantial career success (and not, say, nineteen-year-old students), an urban reader might share in my surprise to encounter such overwhelming concern for how their further successes or failures might project onto their parents. It is striking that their fear of failure at election time had more to do with their parents than themselves and their own peers.

In this and other regards the family in Atlantic Canada can be thought of as a sort of corporate unit. Every success or failure, every compliment or slur reflects on the entire family. In this environment running or not running is truly a decision for the entire extended family. According to one woman who had been elected at the provincial level,

> It takes its toll on your family. I think it was harder on my mother than on my children. My mother used to get furious at anything negative. If you got negative press or the opposition was hounding you, it was water rolling off my back, but she was just devastated. It was just wicked.

Another woman described her husband's reaction to the 'dirty politics' that she encountered while running for municipal office:

When I was going door to door, [my opponent] actually followed me around, and he'd go to the houses right after I went. I'm not going into some of the statements – innuendos and things about myself and my personal life – that I used to hear. Finally, my husband told the fellow, 'Look, if I hear you say one thing more against my wife, you're going to be in court. She's not doing it to you; don't you do it to her.' After that he either stopped or was very careful about who he said it to. But [my opponent] would whine and lie about his financial situation, and if he didn't get a job [as municipal councillor], he was losing his house.

It is interesting to compare this interviewee's reaction with that of her husband. While she was taken aback by the ferocity of the incumbent's campaign to keep his seat, she remained relatively sanguine about the outcome. She described a debate that she had waged with the local media, to refer to her as the 'defeated candidate,' rather than the 'losing candidate,' due to the negative connotations of the latter. She said, 'I had the most wonderful experience. I might not have got elected, but I was not the loser here.' In contrast, her husband's reaction could be considered excessive. Defamation of character and libel are difficult charges to establish under most circumstances, and more difficult still during election campaigns where freedom of speech is paramount. One wonders whether the interviewee's husband would have threatened to sue the opponent if he himself had been the candidate.

We have seen how politics are often taken to project onto the family. It can work the other way around as well. In communities with stable populations and minimal in-migration from away, there is less privacy than in an urban setting. Respondents said there are no secrets for media muckrakers to reveal because everybody already knows everyone else's secrets. One aspiring candidate said coyly, 'Heck, they [the voters] know everyone I've ever slept with.' Similarly in another group, the editor of a small-town newspaper pointed out that 'journalists don't have to dig up the mud because everyone knows it, and nobody ever forgets it.' To this another woman replied, 'It's not just your mud either. It's your father's mud; it's your mother's mud.' The implication is that rural politicians are held responsible for the behaviour of all their family members, even that of their parents before them.

A speaker at another meeting recalled growing up in the spotlight as the daughter of a rural cabinet minister, and contrasted that experience with her later work in urban politics. Her comments capture both senses of the interaction between rural politics and family:

> It is a rural thing. [In the city] I worked [on the campaign team] with John Politician who is a [city] member and people in [the city] don't even know who their members are. Come election time, they are out looking to see who is running, and they don't have a clue. There is no constituency work; there are no events. In a rural district, when my father was a member, my mother worked in the post office, and the things she didn't hear, the things that were told to her and behind her back – it's just completely different. And any time a member goes into a club, it's expected that he buy all the beer. And if the member's children did anything – good, bad, indifferent, or wrong – it was all over town, and you had this special status, your entire family did, because of the fact that the person you were associated with was an elected member. And you were considered open fodder.

Having characterized the intersection between family and politics as a distinctly rural effect, she went on to describe how it has impacted her own electoral ambitions and plans: 'I was a child of a politician. I would never do that to my children, not while they're [young].' All the same, she could not have been altogether bitter about her political childhood because she continued to be politically active behind the scenes in the party's backrooms, and she made a point of not ruling out running for office when her children were older.

The interview excerpts presented above exemplify how the participants conveyed the sense of the individual as not just responsible for herself, but also as a bearer of the family's collective reputation. This characteristic can be seen as a natural outgrowth of living in a stable community populated by the same families that settled them centuries ago. The responsibility of representing the family as a corporate unit creates an extra burden that can, in some cases, deter electoral ambitions.

The Family Vote

Conceptualizing the family as a corporate unit puts us squarely in the territory of the Atlantic Canadian tradition of the 'family vote.' This tradition holds that parents pass their partisan loyalty on to their children, as a core part of the family's identity, embedded in a given community with its particular linguistic and ethnic heritage, and thereby contribute to the durability of a two-party system of competition between Grits and Tories that has prevailed in this region more than elsewhere in Canada, dating back to before Confederation in 1867.

One of the starkest examples of this regional stereotype was presented by an interviewee in her early thirties who recalled her first election after marrying into a highly partisan and politically active family:

> I remember the first time I was married in the family, and there was an election going on. They literally came to get me and said, 'You are going to vote this way.' I said, 'I don't think so. I don't tell you how I'm voting; I haven't told my parents; I'm not telling my husband.' But because the community was small enough, at the end of the vote, they knew how I voted, and how everybody else voted. They came to me and said, 'You voted this way.' And I said, 'How do you know that? You're not supposed to know that.'
>
> Politics was the man's thing. It was the one time of the year when alcohol was brought to the middle of the kitchen table, everybody had a drink and when they talked about it outside the barn. When you got married, it was, 'We've got another [specified party] vote.' They counted in their community how many people voted [for the specified party]. Women would just vote the same way. That was so foreign to my upbringing and the way I was taught to vote – where you listen and where you decide on your own.

This woman's in-laws were electoral officials, so they could identify the one, new additional vote in a small poll where partisanship was stable. The ability of poll captains and scrutineers to track down and identify the newcomer's vote brings to mind stories told in the 1920s soon after women were enfranchised; but judging from this woman's age, it probably happened around 1990. This young bride was shocked to discover that this family did not agree with her perception of the vote as a private, personal preference, but rather considered it to be an expression of corporate solidarity. This sort of family baggage makes partisanship emotionally charged in a way that would be rare in urban Canada where voting preferences tend to fluctuate from one election campaign to another.

The same topic was brought up at several other meetings, but rarely with such gravity. More commonly, it provoked fond bemusement rather than dismay. There was much laughter, for example, at this comment from Newfoundland:

> There are people who are voting because their mom votes that way just because they want to go to Sunday dinner every weekend. It's like, 'We can't

tell Mom that we voted NDP or we're not coming for Jigg's dinner.' And Jigg's dinner is *so* good.

Even if the family vote is rarely enforced rigidly, that it was brought up so often suggests that it remains a common source of approval and disapproval in rural Atlantic Canada. While few, if any, of the rural leaders interviewed would let their families tell them how to vote, they knew which party was favoured, and that constitutes an element of soft coercion that can be expected to influence average voting behaviour when viewed over a distribution of voters.

Soft coercion can take on a harder edge when the focus shifts from the private act of voting to the public sphere: joining a party, campaigning for it, or running as a candidate. One interviewee recalled that when she was an NDP candidate in rural Nova Scotia, a relative admonished her: 'Your grandfathers would roll over in their graves if they knew.' The implication is that everyone in the community could see her promoting a non-traditional party, and this public act would reflect badly on her forebears. Given the solicitude for the reputation of parents reported in the preceding section, it is not difficult to see how joining, or running for, the 'wrong' political party could be seen as a disloyal act towards one's family, even among educated, and politically active women. An analogy can be drawn to the social convention that family members attend the same church; considerably more latitude is extended to what an individual believes spiritually than to where they worship in public.

It takes more of a logical leap to see how the family vote could affect the overall level of women's participation in public life. If voting and campaigning for a political party is an act of corporate solidarity within the extended family, could not standing as a candidate also be an act of solidarity? It is logically plausible to imagine women – even young daughters-in-law – pursuing their political ambitions within a paradigm of family solidarity. If all the political parties were equally hospitable or inhospitable to women's leadership, a convention that a family support the same party would not be a barrier. By analogy, if all churches were identical, the social convention to attend the family church would not be a barrier to women's spiritual and administrative involvement. But just as all churches are not identical, neither are all political parties. It is well established that one party – the NDP – has historically nurtured women's leadership, has run more female candidates, and has elected proportionally more women, than have the other major parties, including the two traditionally dominant parties in Atlantic Canada – the Liberals and

Conservatives (Young and Campbell 2001, 66–7, 71–2). Indeed, previous literature has proposed a linkage between the low proportions of women elected in Atlantic Canada and the relative inability of the NDP to establish a viable beachhead beyond Halifax (Matland and Studlar 1998). In this section we see the beginnings of an understanding of the magnitude of the electoral challenge facing a non-traditional political party in rural Atlantic Canada.

An anecdote from the interviews exemplifies the perverse dynamics that can arise in the NDP's attempts to gain a foothold in rural Atlantic Canada:

> And heaven help a divorced woman if she wants to run for politics! It prevented me from running because I was courted by the NDP to run last year. I was going through a divorce at the time. It was one of the factors when we sat down and talked about my candidacy and about how it would look in the community. [My divorce] was one of the factors that came forward; it wasn't the deciding factor in why I didn't run, but it was one of the first factors that came up in that discussion, the very first. I didn't bring it up. And this is the NDP, where we're not supposed to be like that.

This anecdote brings to mind the old joke about refusing to join any club that would take someone like you as a member, except that here it appears in the converse. This woman's breaking with her husband's family (and its voting preferences) presumably played a part in her availability as a candidate in a non-traditional party. Yet the local NDP executive felt that this same non-traditional characteristic (being divorced) would make her less electable, as she would not lend the party the veneer of conventional respectability that it judged was needed. This anecdote seems especially ironic considering that the NDP has historically led the way in defending diversity, and that the party leader at the time (Alexa McDonough), and the previous leader (Audrey McLaughlin), are both divorced women.

While the influence of the family vote may be declining in rural Atlantic Canada, as it has been across the country, the comments of the interviewees suggest that it remains a topic of discussion and a persistent element of soft coercion. It should be remembered from Chapter 3 that the interviewees are as a group well educated and well employed, and it seems reasonable to infer an independent mindedness that insulates them from their families' preferences. Perhaps not coincidentally, a higher proportion of participants reported support for the NDP than would be found in a random sample in their communities. The analysis presented here relates the family vote to the challenges encountered by the NDP in rural Atlantic Canada. This is not meant to propose that the family vote is a root cause for electoral inertia, based on cultural or ethnic distinctions, but rather, that it is a mechanism that helps to maintain the inertia. Why is there a preferred political party in the first place? Further interview results presented in later chapters will shed light on systemic and economic forces that underpin the predilection for electoral solidarity, without resting on culture and ethnicity.

Family Legacies of Power and Influence

If your actions can reflect back on your forebears, it stands to reason that their earlier successes and distinctions can carry forward to grace you. Indeed, Jane Arscott noted a stereotypical pattern in Atlantic Canada of incumbency spanning the generations, with sons 'inheriting' their father's seats in virtual family fiefdoms (1997). Several high-profile examples of this phenomenon have subsequently emerged. In 2003 Peter MacKay won the leadership of the national Progressive Conservative Party, having been first elected in 1997 as the representative in the House of Commons for Pictou-Antigonish-Guysborough, Nova Scotia. His father, Elmer MacKay, held that same seat[2] from 1971 to 1988 and served in the cabinet of the Conservative government of Brian Mulroney. Similarly, Dominic LeBlanc was elected in 2000 as the Liberal member of Parliament for Beauséjour-Petitcodiac, New Brunswick. His father, Romeo LeBlanc, held that same seat from 1972 to 1984, before being appointed to the Senate and then as governor general of Canada, in 1994. In 2002 Shawn Graham became the leader of the Liberal Party of New Brunswick, having been first elected to the provincial legislature in 1998 to represent the riding of Kent, the same seat held earlier by his father, Alan Graham, who also was a provincial cabinet minister. In 2003 Robert Ghiz was elected leader of the Liberal Party of Prince Edward Island, a position that had been held from 1981 to 1996 by his father, Joseph Ghiz, former premier of P.E.I. Federal Liberal MP Geoff Regan and Nova Scotia Liberal MLA (and former party leader) Danny Graham are two more examples of young men taking up the family 'business' of politics in Atlantic Canada.

In the present study, family legacies of power and prestige were brought up for discussion by interviewees at most of the meetings. In the following excerpt, a postsecondary college instructor claimed that family pedigree was just as important as formal education in preparing politicians in her province:

INSTRUCTOR: Newfoundland is very traditional in the sense of the 'haves and have-nots,' like the merchants and the fishermen, and that has always carried on throughout our history of the province, and it still is, as a matter of fact. I grew up in Cornerbrook, which is a very company-oriented town, where the traditional families who had money, like the [family name specified], or if you're in Grand Falls, the [second family name specified]. Whichever part of the province you're in, there are particular families, that even though their legacy is now a historical legacy, the name still carries a certain amount of power with it. And if you didn't come from that side of the ...
SPEAKER 1: I came from a family with a mother who ... I mean I'm a bastard child. Imagine that, I'm at the end of the world, who's going to vote for me?
INSTRUCTOR: And even now in Newfoundland, though I love to think that we are making big steps forward, moving away from [family lineage making] a difference to people. You don't perhaps want to put yourself out where people are going to talk about your family, or talk about the skeletons in the closet. Or you just think, 'I'm not as good as whichever family it is.'

Legacies of power and influence only work, of course, when the population is stable enough to recognize which families to defer to, and such traditional patterns of deference survive only because there is little migration into rural Atlantic Canada. A system of family lineage is, of course, non-democratic, verging on aristocratic. But it does not automatically exclude women. The instructor quoted above went on to cite the well-known case of the former leader of Newfoundland's Conservatives as an example of how women can benefit from family lineage, just as men do:

Lynn Verge[3] was a Fisher, one of the Fisher family, and they were really well known. So there is a still a certain amount of prestige that is always required. I hope that we are moving away from that, but I do think that certainly tainted the picture previously, and I'm sure that it still remains.

A Nova Scotia group cited former MLA Eleanor Norrie in this regard: 'She had the money, contacts, family name [her mother-in-law was a senator]. A lot of it is who you know, as well as the money.'[4] Established families have wives, sisters, daughters, and daughters-in-law, any of whom could have political interests and ambitions. Assuming they have the other conventional resources that equip them to take up leadership roles, we see that an established family name can work to the advantage of women, just as it can for men.

The topic of sons and daughters in influential families came up at another meeting, in an area where a son had 'inherited' his father's seat. The conversation began when one participant (who is a member of the competing party) said, 'If your dog was a [politician's last name specified], he would win.' When I explicitly asked why none of the women in that family were candidates, participants displayed a detailed knowledge about the internal workings of the family.

SPEAKER 1: Well John Jr said himself that his sister should have run because she was much more enthusiastic than he was. He said that she was just keyed up for his election, 'She wants me to run so bad.'
SPEAKER 2: Yeah, but why wouldn't she run?
SPEAKER 3: Her exact words were she wanted to get her career started.
SPEAKER 4: Trouble is John Jr's father John was in power for twenty-seven years and John Jr worked for his father. He was groomed by his Dad. He was his right-hand man, and when his Dad decided to resign, John Jr stepped in to run. He was the only one of the children that was interested in politics. Or made that much of an interest to work with his Dad in whatever. And then John Jr ran and got in the party.
SPEAKER 2: But I wonder if John Jr really wants to make politics his career, because we've heard different things.

In this case, the daughter claimed not to be interested in taking up the family mantle. The interviewee, through her tone, conveyed scepticism about the daughter's frankness, but did not elaborate on her feelings about whether the daughter really wanted to run or whether she had some other reason for not running. There will always be a distribution of aptitudes, and many daughters would not be interested in politics; but overall, roughly equal proportions of sons and daughters could logically be expected to be interested in politics. As it turns out, in this case, there was indeed a daughter in a different family who was interested in being nominated:

SPEAKER 1: Before John Jr accepted the party's nomination, there was a woman who was very capable, had two young children, and who had been approached to run and would have run, except the party wanted the Politician name. And they practically twisted John Jr's arm, and he will say himself that the premier called him every day for a week. So [the woman above] stepped aside.

The interviewee proceeded to explain that even though this particular woman had a well-known father with a respected name, it was not as highly regarded as the Politician family name, which the party thought it needed to guarantee the seat in a tightly contested election. One wonders whose name would have prevailed had John Jr's sister stood against the aspiring woman's brother for the nomination. Of course, we can never know the answer to this hypothetical question, but the ramifications for women's leadership are not insignificant, considering the prominent role that the reluctant John Jr went on to play in Atlantic politics.

As a contrasting example, an interviewee at another meeting did manage to win the nomination for her party. She claimed that the advantage of a family name gave her a leg-up campaigning in a provincial election because most of the voters knew and acknowledged her father as a community leader:

> But again at a rural level for women, it's when you knock on doors. Again when you look at the age of our community, if they don't remember me, then [they'll ask] 'Whose daughter are you? Well [since] you're John Politician's daughter and you are here campaigning, then that's okay.' But [if I weren't John Politician's daughter they would have said,] 'What do you mean you weren't born here? Well exactly how long have you been here?' That would be the next question.

In this woman's case, her credibility as a serious candidate was already established by her status as the 'daughter of.' For her, family lineage was simply one more resource, in addition to the standard socioeconomic resources of education, income, and political knowledge that contributed to her civic engagement. Nevertheless, it is worth noting that she lost the election to the long-time incumbent (representing another major party), who was a man.

The issue of incumbency plays a central role in determining how quickly the proportions of women elected can change. Women tend to benefit from an electoral system in which incumbency is low, and the recruitment pool is flexible and fluid, owing to the historical preponderance of male incumbents. The situation in rural Atlantic Canada may be mathematically similar to that in the U.S. Congress, where high incumbency or low turnover has been identified as an important factor in women's lower rates of electoral success at the national level. In theory, a high turnover rate would shake up electoral outcomes and allow newcomers of all sorts, including women, to contest open-seat elections more competitively. Discussions in later chapters will identify systemic obstacles to reducing incumbency in rural Atlantic Canada.

Legacies of family power and control can effect electoral inertia beyond directly holding elected office within the family. A group of particularly well-heeled and influential middle-aged interviewees at one meeting spoke of a more indirect influence on the choice of candidates in their communities:

SPEAKER 1: It's driven by that power of the overseers that do not want to see new blood, new representation, new ideas or change come into the picture.

SPEAKER 2: A lot of it doesn't have to do with politics. It has to do with personal, holding-onto – control. They have their agenda that has nothing to do with politics. They simply don't like the person. Or they thought the person would go down the tubes, and they found out that they don't. The better you do, the worse they like you. If they don't like you, they try to put obstacles in your path.

Others at the same meeting spoke of a more pervasive influence that goes beyond elected office:

SPEAKER 3: Every community has – how do I put it? – a history of people who control things.

SPEAKER 4: They are the families who came up through, who had money, basically.

SPEAKER 3: Fathers of the community so-called. [They say,] 'Don't forget who really got you that job you're at today. Don't forget who got your son that position over there.' These are the people that control the community overall. No, it's not just through money. They control through years of pass-me-down-through-generations control. There are families in [this county], everybody knows the [names of specific families]. It will always be there. Once they start feeling that they are losing control that's been brought through the generations, once they start seeing change, new ideas, or that something could actually happen and that person might actually get credit for it, then they start losing grip on the power, and then it's easy to say, 'Alright, You're on that board, what are they trying to do down there? We should try to stop that. That isn't good.' That's how it works.

In general, it is not unusual to hear people in many settings grumble about conspiracies and inner circles of power. But it is important to understand that all of the interviewees quoted above are exceptionally privileged and involved in local public life, even compared with those who participated at other meetings. I was surprised to hear such wealthy and successful women use the term 'overseers' with its connotations of slave plantations. Why would these women speak so matter of factly about the oppressive power of an 'establishment'? Were they not part of it? In fact, when Speaker 3 above listed the surnames of families who exert control in her community, some of them were the same surnames as those of other women sitting at the table! The participants at this meeting had grown up in the community, gone to school with, dated, and in some cases married the very same 'overseers' who were said to control the community. Perhaps being closer to the centre of power has made them more sensitive and acutely aware than most. The disdain expressed by these women for what they describe as an oppressive environment will emerge as a recurrent theme in later chapters.

The control that these so-called overseers exert over the choice of candidates evokes the concept of the gatekeeper. Janine Brodie (1977) found that even women who had been candidates as long ago as 1945 emphasized the role of local party elites who could make or break a woman's political career. Sources regularly cite the 'old-boys' network,' particularly at the level of the local riding association, as being reluctant to nominate women as party candidates and as being unsupportive of those who are elected. Informal power struggles and unspoken assumptions about the nature of leadership are particularly important in the Canadian context given that the candidate selection process is extremely decentralized. Local elites zealously stake out their turf in which to operate without obstructions, on the principle that local democracy overrides almost any consideration, including gender parity.[5] Gatekeeping is not synonymous with generalized sexism, but rather, it is inseparable from the solidarity that characterizes Canadian political parties, and it underpins party discipline in legislatures. Gatekeepers make or break the careers of men, and it can go either way for women too.

One of the prime mechanisms for exerting influence over the choice of candidates is through campaign finance. The 1991 Royal Commission on Electoral Reform and Party Financing brought attention to campaign issues, and in its final report stressed that the low proportion of women elected was, in part, determined by their lack of access to sources of campaign funds (113–15). This problem is especially acute at the nomination stage of the process, which, at the time of the interviews, was not regulated by provincial or federal law.[6] A party's official sources of funding, some of which are exclusively directed to women, become available only after an aspiring candidate wins the nomination and becomes that party's official candidate.

One of the interviewees in this study described this very barrier at the nomination stage. She did go on to win the nomination, and the seat, and eventually was appointed to cabinet. But that first step was particularly precarious:

> You are totally on your own in a nomination. There is no party support for you because they should not favour a candidate, so it is only the few friends that gather around you. It's not income tax deductible, so it is just out of somebody's pocket. Getting through the nomination is one of the most difficult things because you are on your own within your own party. And among your friends, too, you're basically on your own. But once you get past [the nomination], then your bagman (in my case it was a man) takes over, and he goes to all the businesses. I came out of my election not owing anything. But the nomination, I tell you, was a crucifixion ... Everything was my expense until I passed the nomination – then I couldn't believe how the money came in, it was like magic.

This woman had self-funded the bulk of the expenses for her first nomination campaign, which she estimated to have cost her $50,000 in savings and lost wages. As the campaign went on for a year, she took unpaid leave from work, and this had a negative impact on her pension from that job. Only after she won the nomination and became the official candidate, did the party's regular donors step in to fund her campaign

Aspiring women candidates in rural areas may be more vulnerable to campaign finance barriers than women in urban centres, for two reasons. One participant pointed out that transportation costs for campaign workers doing signage were higher, because of the large distances involved and the high cost of automobile fuel in these areas of Atlantic Canada. But she also claimed an additional cultural dimension to the expense: 'And you're expected to feed [supporters] too, so the nomination day itself is quite expensive. Whereas in a city – because I am involved in nominations in the capital city as well – there is no such thing, other than a little party afterwards.' The general claim that rural nominations are more expensive may seem rather implausible, considering reports of lavish nomination campaigns at the national level in major Canadian cities. But the speaker was comparing the situation with provincial nominations in St John's, which may be more modest.

In any case, it is indisputably more difficult to raise funds in rural Atlantic Canada than in a major urban or suburban riding. Moreover, few participants demonstrated a real understanding of how fundraising works, as nomination expenses are perhaps the most opaque part of the electoral process. Even respondents who had worked on election campaigns were, for the most part, less sophisticated about financing nomination bids than about other aspects of the process. When asked directly, most interviewees said that they have extensive networks of friends who they could call on to volunteer and raise funds for a political cause or a nomination campaign, but that they do not feel comfortable raising money for themselves, for fear of appearing to be selfish. One young woman who held an official extra-parliamentary position in a major political party said, 'I wouldn't have the gall to go to a business that was either Tory or Liberal or NDP or whatever and ask for a donation.'

Participants who had actually run as candidates tend to view the above formulation of the fundraising process (in terms of asking around for money) as more of an indication of naïveté than as a real barrier.

> Although parties are not supposed to give the official nod to anyone [prior to choosing an official candidate], they often do. They give the unofficial, under-the-table nod, which puts many resources to the candidate that they, in particular, are interested in having the nomination. If you don't happen to be that candidate, then you are screwed.

This comment suggests that regular big donors for political parties sometimes begin to leak money to their favoured candidate before the party makes the official selection. Unless an aspiring candidate is on the receiving side of this largesse, how would she know who was quietly funding whom during the nomination campaign?

Other participants made it clear that this sort of dynamic is not restricted to partisan politics. One interviewee related her surprise at how easy it was to finance her mayoralty bid:

> I don't want you to be under the assumption that you can exist without your bagman, without him asking and begging. I tell you this, when I ran for

mayor, it was a thousand dollars just dropped in cash, even before I said I
was running – that was the nod that I should run.

This woman had not needed to self-fund her own mayoralty campaign,
nor ask around for funds, because the cash had just appeared from
sources who wanted her elected.

In the absence of regulation, nobody really knows what happens during the initial stage of candidacy, and even the aspiring candidates may
not know where their funds come from. This is when politicians are most
vulnerable to the vagaries and whims of funding availability. The above
comments from the interviewees show that wealthy and powerful people
from leading families sometimes intervene, quietly and anonymously, at
this stage, to provide much-needed resources to their favoured candidate. They illuminate one of the mechanisms by which gatekeepers exert
their influence in rural Atlantic Canada.

Summary

This chapter reports interviewees' perceptions of the interaction
between their family life and their community involvement. Participants
described an environment of pervasive intimacy, in which family relationships intersect and spill over into every walk of life, including politics. High expectations for extended-family relations introduce the
potential for gender-role time constraints, especially given that interviewees perceive the role of a rural politician to be particularly onerous.
Despite its logical appeal, however, among these interviewees the time
constraint itself did not emerge as a significant barrier to running for
elected office. Interviewees frequently attributed this deterrent to other
women in the hypothetical abstract, but not directly to themselves. If
anything, the interview groups tended to feature a certain competitiveness among these energetic women, in terms of their willingness and
ability to cope with time demands, and the accommodations they have
reached with their husbands and families in order to continue with their
civic engagement.

Moving beyond basic time constraints, interviewees also described a
different sort of burden, in which every success or failure that they
encounter, and every compliment or slur, is taken to reflect on the entire
family. Articulating this sense of heightened responsibility led to a characterization of the family as a kind of corporate unit. In this environment
decisions about running for elected office are not individual choices.

Some interviewees found that this burden deterred their own electoral ambitions.

A related concept discussed in the interviews is the tradition of the family vote, in which parents pass their partisan loyalty on to their children, as a core part of the family's identity. While it is no longer enforced rigidly, that the family vote was brought up so often suggests that it remains a common source of approval and disapproval in rural Atlantic Canada – an element of soft coercion that may have an impact on average voting behaviour. Soft coercion can take on a harder edge when the focus shifts from the private act of voting to the public sphere. Running as a candidate for, or even joining, the wrong political party is perceived as a greater act of disloyalty, and some interviewees, especially those involved with the NDP, encountered strong resistance from their families.

Interviewees also discussed family legacies of power and influence, with sons 'inheriting' their father's seats in virtual family fiefdoms. Many interviewees agreed that family pedigree continues to be a significant factor in the choice of political candidates. Examples were given of women politicians benefiting from their family name, but the stories more commonly involved men. Interviewees' opinions of this tradition were overwhelmingly negative; even relatively privileged women who were close to the centre of power expressed disdain for what they saw as an oppressive system controlled by 'overseers.'

One of the prime mechanisms for exerting influence over the choice of candidates is through campaign finance. Candidates are most vulnerable at the nomination stage, before their party's official sources of funding become available. Interviewees described campaigns in which regular donors began to leak money to their favoured candidate before the party made the official selection.

6 The Slushy Intersection between Politics and Occupation

A rural woman's job defines how she spends a good deal of her time, perhaps second only to her family. If she has paid employment, as do most of the interviewees in this study, some of her most important relationships are with the colleagues, customers, and clients she encounters at work. These activities and relationships have significant ramifications for her participation in public affairs outside of her home or workplace. It is a truism in the study of political behaviour that occupation is a key socioeconomic resource on which people draw to exercise power in a liberal democracy. The skills and networks built up in the course of pursuing one's occupation can translate into basic qualifications for many public responsibilities, depending on the nature of the occupation. As one well-placed interviewee put it,

> someone just doesn't arrive with the executive decision-making skills to be an effective MP or cabinet minister. You learn those [skills] in the jobs you had previously, and most of those are executive-type jobs, where you lead and make decisions, and delegate. Most of those jobs are dominated by men, so that's yet another difficulty because most women work in sectors that have different decision-making styles, where it's a flatter hierarchy, or they are at the bottom of the hierarchy. Women just don't have access to those kinds of hierarchical jobs, and if you look at the women who have been hand-picked [to run by the party leader], they are the ones who have had those kinds of [hierarchical] jobs.

We will see from other interviewees that one's job can also present barriers. This chapter discusses some of the ways in which interviewees perceived their jobs as affecting their participation in public affairs and political aspirations.

Remnants of the Public Service Prohibition against Partisan Involvement

Public sector jobs have been described as the backbone of the Atlantic economy. A study by the Canadian Institute for Research on Regional Development (Beaudin 1998, 46–7) found that in 1995 public sector jobs contribute 35 per cent of employment income in the Maritimes, compared with an average of 27 per cent across Canada. These jobs have more of an impact than the number of people employed might indicate, especially in rural areas, because the public sector tends to hire qualified, educated people on a permanent, year-round basis. Their regular paycheques insulate local businesses from the vagaries of seasonal employment in other industries such as fishing and tourism. Public sector employment has been a primary route through which women have acquired leadership skills and resources for more than a century. Such empowerment was evident among the women studied in this project. Recall that the results in chapter 3 show that the big-budget fields of education, health care, and social services employ disproportionate numbers of the interviewees – as teachers, nurses, and social service workers, among other professions.

Ironically, public sector employment has historically also been a barrier for translating those skills and resources associated with one's job into the exercise of real power. Until the mid-1980s, in all four Atlantic provinces it was illegal for provincial government employees to publicly support one political party over another or to run for public office under a party label. Formal legal prohibitions against partisan involvement by public sector employees have since been lifted across Canada, in compliance with freedom-of-association rights guaranteed by the Charter of Rights and Freedoms. For example, Nova Scotia revoked the prohibition in 1987 by amending section 38 of the Civil Service Act, amid considerable controversy. Since the laws against partisan involvement were repealed some time ago, and since in the first place they only applied to direct employees of the federal or provincial governments, one might infer that many public sector workers outside the provincial and federal governments were never inhibited from entering politics by their jobs, and that those who were are no longer so inhibited. However, we will see that this is not the case.

It would be more accurate to say that the legal prohibitions were merely formal manifestations of a much more broadly applied and widely held principle of staying above politics and that this principle persists to varying degrees throughout the public sector. A telling example illustrates this interpretation rather elegantly. At one meeting, a retired Nova Scotia teacher recalled, with a tone of regret in her voice, that

> when I was teaching, when my husband was teaching, you weren't allowed to be politically active. At one time, you could not run for political office and that stays with you.

It seems that this interviewee was unaware that teachers were never covered by the provincial legislation prohibiting partisanship, as they are not directly employed by the provincial government. While this error would be understandable among disinterested members of the general public, it is surprising when it comes from this woman, herself a teacher and experienced community leader. Her skewed recollection speaks volumes about a deeply held principle pervading the public sector that has trumped the letter of the law for a long time.

A high-profile example of the persistence of this principle within the government of Nova Scotia occurred in 1997 when Peter MacKay sought the Conservative nomination for Pictou-Antigonish-Guysborough, in preparation for the Canadian general election held later that year. When he made his intentions public, the Nova Scotia Liberal government threatened to fire him from his job as provincial Crown attorney (Alberts 2003). MacKay stayed the course (and went on eventually to lead the PC Party to its merger with the Canadian Alliance Party in 2003) – and the Nova Scotia government made good its threat.

Considering how many among the pool of qualified women work in the public sector, it stands to reason that an ongoing informal prohibition on partisanship might have a substantial impact on women's exercise of power. Indeed, interviewees at several meetings attested to the persistence of an unwritten prohibition in the public sector against visible political partisanship:

> I know that there are people in this province who considered running for political parties, and were pretty much told, 'If you run, you'll never have that job again.' People who have government ties ... People who hold those kind of jobs [working in government and on government-funded projects] are at risk because the people who are in power can say, 'You can run for office, but if you do – even if you lose – you will lose your job and you will never get that job back again.'

To this interviewee, verbal threats and intimidation have replaced the legal prohibition.

Other interviewees were more circumspect, while conveying similar ideas. At one meeting an economic development officer who works at a Regional Economic Development Agency (REDA) was asked if she would feel comfortable running for elected office. In response, she threw her hands up in mock horror and said facetiously, 'No, honestly I didn't even vote in the last election,' as a caricature of her required pretence of neutrality. One might think her partisanship should be irrelevant because she works for a county-level or municipal government, which is non-partisan. However, she explained that REDAs are funded by all three levels of government, and so she perceived her partisanship to be a matter of some sensitivity.

The not-for-profit sector[1] of the economy can be considered to be part of the public sector, broadly defined, and similar conventions were found to apply here too. This category refers to organizations that rely almost exclusively on government funding. The most visible and familiar examples are social services agencies (such as women's shelters, food banks, and counselling and rehabilitation centres) which receive a renewable, block grant from government and operate at arm's-length. In their capacity as public sector entrepreneurs,[2] women interviewed in this study who direct non-government social services agencies expressed concerns about the precariousness of their positions, perhaps to an even greater degree than the women who are directly employed by the government did. For example, the executive director of one social service agency justified her personal conviction that she should stay well away from politics:

> I don't think anyone would ask me to run because I am dealing with sexuality. It is too controversial. Plus it might be a deterrent to our organization because we really depend on public support. We wouldn't want to be perceived as being aligned with any one political party.

Unlike government employees, public sector entrepreneurs and other employees in the not-for-profit sector do not have the benefit of provincial labour law or the protection of a collective agreement that includes provisions for political leave. Instead, their funding can be revoked without recourse at the end of each budgetary year. As a result, they quite justifiably worry that the agency's credibility might be jeopardized if they were to become involved in partisan politics.

There are exceptions, of course, and whether to be openly partisan is a matter for each individual's personal judgment based on her reading of her own unique vulnerabilities. Sharon Whelan, executive director of the Bay St George Women's Centre, ran as an NDP candidate in the 1999 provincial election. After being defeated she continued as executive director at the Women's Centre, with funding from the (Liberal) provincial government and the (Liberal) federal government. Her case appears to be exceptional, however, as no other examples were encountered of such cavalier disregard for potentially negative repercussions.

Officials with the Nova Scotia Advisory Council on the Status of Women, as well as those with Status of Women Canada, confirmed these interview results, suggesting that an unwritten prohibition on partisanship continues to inhibit women's leadership among public sector employees. These officials felt that obvious partisanship forms a barrier to their own work in the field to promote 'capacity building' or 'empowerment.' They expressed frustration that their efforts to promote women's leadership have typically operated within a circumscribed notion of capacity or empowerment as psychological, occupational, and relational. At some point, they felt that empowering women must necessarily involve positions of power, which in a liberal democracy, are associated with partisan politics. Yet they had to skate on thin ice to provide guidance or advice to any woman who was engaged in partisan activities, for fear of appearing to endorse one political party over another.

An interesting distinction arose when these same NSACSW officials described how they were personally affected by the prohibition outside their own jobs. While acknowledging that they were effectively restricted from campaigning for or endorsing any party, they characterized their non-partisanship as a matter of professional principle and expressed a personal pride in adhering to this principle. We could attribute the difference to the relatively high standing that these officials held within the public service. Yet that same personal pride in the professional principle of neutrality was encountered frequently among the interviewees. Women employed in either category – both public sector employees and not-for-profit entrepreneurs – feel that it is inappropriate for them personally to be involved in partisan politics or even to express a partisan preference. This suggests that the remnants of the prohibition go deeper than just verbal or implied threats from those who control the purse strings. To the extent that it has been internalized by the employees themselves, as part of the professional ethos in the public sector, this barrier becomes all the more formidable.

For the foreseeable future, the public sector will continue to have a significant presence in rural Atlantic Canada, and it will continue to employ or fund many of the region's professional women. They are already leaders in non-partisan civic affairs, serving on local government boards and providing a good deal of the work in voluntary organizations. A prohibition against partisanship, whether or not it is backed up by law, skims off much of the cream of local talent at the outset of the recruitment process, to the impoverishment of electoral democracy. Governance includes partisanship, and it seems perverse to promote 'women's leadership' and 'women's empowerment' while cutting them off at the knees.

The Classroom as Leadership Training Ground

While remnants of the old prohibition against partisanship persist throughout much of the public sector, one public sector occupation has embraced politics with vigour. Interviewees in all four Atlantic provinces indicated that teachers have emerged as an important supply of political candidates at both the municipal and provincial levels.

One interaction that prompted me to recognize the role of teachers was a redirection of my line of inquiry by the interviewees at a meeting with the Women's Institute executive in Prince Edward Island. I noted that some of the first women to be elected in that province – Marion Reid, Leone Bagnall, and Marion Murphy – were WI members, and I wondered whether that experience had something to do with their success. One interviewee agreed that there was an indirect connection: 'I think if you are a WI member you learn a lot about leadership. It is an educational organization to belong to. You gain confidence. You start local and then you move and move and move.' However, another woman pointed out a different pattern that she felt was equally relevant: 'They were also schoolteachers. The three of them.' This observation led me to review the occupational backgrounds of current women MLAs in PEI. Indeed, I found that the pattern had continued: two of the six women who held seats at the time of the interviews (Pat Mella and Mildred Dover, both cabinet ministers) had been teachers before entering politics, and another teacher (Carolyn Bertram) was elected in 2003, along with incumbent Mildred Dover.

The prominence of teachers in politics was noted in other provinces as well. At a meeting in Nova Scotia, the first woman elected to municipal council in her community related a change that she perceived on council after her tenure:

When the law was changed in 1987 so that they could run, the teachers all decided, 'We'll run and we'll change things.' So that's what they do.

This interviewee shared the same misconception about the legal status of teachers as the teacher cited in the preceding section. A non-teacher herself, she described the subsequent influx of teachers as exerting a dominant force on municipal council. (It should be noted that she was not very enthusiastic about having so many teachers on municipal council; instead, she advocated a dominant role for the business community.) She did not see the influx of teachers as having yet impacted the number of women on council in her own community, because both male and female teachers had entered the municipal forum. Nevertheless, the fact that women are overrepresented among teachers suggests the potential for an expanding pathway to the exercise of power by women.

Among the Atlantic provinces, nowhere was the increasingly important role of teachers more strongly articulated than in Newfoundland. Interviewees at all four meetings there reported that teachers were prominent political actors. A PC Party activist who had worked on community economic development projects in various parts of Newfoundland observed:

> The other thing that I find interesting here is that a lot of teachers run. It would be the professional within a lot of the rural communities because the schools are drawing from a larger and larger geographic area so they run through. When you are a teacher for twenty years in a place where you are drawing on all the communities ... you know all the people in that district; you have taught them all. So you have that contact already. A lot of our legislators have been teachers. It does give people the network. They are professionals, so they do have the image, and they are educated, and they move on into it. So from my experience in rural Newfoundland, it is the teachers and not so much the family-run businesses.

It makes sense on a number of levels that teaching should be a practical route to political office. As pointed out by the interviewee quoted above, teachers get to know an enormous number of people through their jobs; not just the students in their classrooms, but their families as well, sometimes over several generations. As a result of rural depopulation, the size of school board districts has expanded, in some cases to nearly the same size as electoral districts. This expansion situates teachers as among the few people who have networks covering almost all prospective voters. Their job also helps them to develop skills in rhetoric, persuasion, and compulsion in the exercise of authority. These networks and skills position teachers as natural leaders in the community.[3]

Such considerations help to explain why teachers in general might have an affinity for politics. Another interviewee provided an explanation for why she believes this is particularly so in Newfoundland. She said that teachers in her community became leaders effectively by default, as a result of a weak economy:

> When I lived in [a small town in Newfoundland] my first big surprise was that you would go to church and you would see very few men. You would go downtown and you would see very few men. And you would wonder what was going on. It took a while, and then I discovered that 90 per cent of the men of that community worked away. A lot of them were gone for nine, ten months of the year, and the women were left to raise the families and run the community, because I found there was a very apathetic sense to the whole community. And that was because there, there was too much else to do, and you didn't have time. The only ones you saw in municipal politics, I think there were only two women there and both were teachers, and men were teachers, that's all that seemed to be.

In some areas, the majority of the population might be consumed by the day–to-day business of cobbling together a subsistence income from diverse and transitory sources. When a fish plant closes, for example, its direct suppliers close, and as unemployment rises, people leave in search of work elsewhere, and local retail ventures shut down. Governments eventually withdraw services to declining communities. Schools, however, are among the last bit of public infrastructure to close down, and teachers are among the last educated professionals with secure incomes to remain in the community.

The Private Sector: Keeping the Peace with Clients, Customers, and Bosses

The economic structure of the rural areas where this research was conducted varies a great deal, from the relatively prosperous – the fruit and dairy farms of the Annapolis Valley, the lobster fishery of Nova Scotia's South Shore, and the public sector services centre of Clarenville – to the less prosperous, the western shore of Newfoundland and Cape Breton. Amid this diversity a general pattern holds of relatively high reliance on the primary resource-extraction industries of farming, fishing, forestry, and mining. As such these rural economies are less diversified than those in major urban centres and their suburban peripheries. Some parts of these private sector industries, principally farming, fishing, and small wood lots, are characterized by household-based enterprises, while others are characterized by large-scale industrial enterprises such as pulp and paper mills or mining operations. The services sector is larger than some people might suppose. It includes business services, for example, insurance brokers and accountants, industrial services such as welding and pipefitting, and consumer services, which are often limited to a few small-scale enterprises such as gas stations and grocers.

Within such an industrial structure, what consequences does private sector employment have for women's leadership in public life? We might expect the answer to this complex question to be most accessible in the case of small-business owners. In Canada, the Conservative and, to a lesser extent, the Liberals, have a long tradition of drawing from the ranks of the local 'petit-bourgeoisie' for their members, campaign workers, and candidates. There are practical reasons why small-business operators would be active in partisan politics. For one thing, these people often have considerable flexibility to take political leave, particularly when they operate a partnership or family firm and other people can step in to fill their shoes. In contrast, very few waged workers (only some members of large unions) have contracts that include provisions for political leave. Moreover, a small business might benefit from the owner's partisan engagement, even beyond the obvious (but now illegal) possibility of preferential award of government contracts. Partisan engagement is a way to network professionally and thus to meet a wider range of potential clients and service providers. A small-business owner's candidacy can provide additional publicity for the enterprise, raising its profile in the area. Looking at the larger picture, many small businesses have a special interest in a political system that is based on geographical electoral districts because their prosperity is closely intertwined with their geographical location. Whereas employees can often relocate to where their skills are in demand, most small-business owners cannot move their business assets such as land, customer base, and reputation. They are therefore usually considered to be committed to the collective long-term prosperity of their town or area in a different way from waged employees, which gives them more of a stake in local political affairs. These considerations led me to expect vigorous partisan engagement by small-business owners in the communities that I would visit.

Interviewees painted a very different picture, however, of the political role of small-business owners in rural Atlantic Canada. While they often spoke of small-business owners participating in local community affairs through municipal office, they also described a nearly universal aversion to partisan politics that is based on a fear of offending clients and customers. One participant in her early thirties talked about her father, who had served as deputy mayor when she was growing up:

SPEAKER 1: My dad had a business for twenty-seven years, and he would never, ever talk [partisan] politics. It was just something that you didn't do because of business. You never wanted to offend anybody; you had to remain very neutral.

SPEAKER 2: When we had the store, Tom would say, 'I tease both sides of the fence just the same.'

SPEAKER 1: Maybe in a rural community, we are getting back to [the idea that] everybody knows everybody and all that. But when I look back on a farmer in comparison to a merchant – as a farmer, you are running your own business, but your sales from other people coming are not dependent on [your opinion]. Dad served all walks of life, and my dad's motto was 'Just be nice.' That was the one thing that, as a kid growing up, he always said. And that was what he preached, be nice – just try and be neutral to everybody. He had a job that relied on people coming into the store, and if you were a controversial person they weren't going to come in the store. They were not going to put bread and milk on the table.

SPEAKER 3: I think in rural Maritimes, politics was a main topic of conversation, and you knew who voted for who, and for a few weeks before the election, you hated the fellow next door because you knew he was a damn you-know-what. And for a couple of days after, you dug him in the ribs with a snarky remark if you wanted and you didn't go to the store for a week. And then everyone was back friends again. But you still knew that the bugger, he voted the other way.

In a low-growth economy where the customer base is static, or even diminishing, it makes sense that small-business owners would not want to take the risk of putting off potential customers in any way. The comments of the interviewees made it clear that partisanship is high on the list of offences in these communities, where the family vote is an act of corporate solidarity, and election campaigns draw firm lines between allies and opponents.

On the lighter side, one respondent related, with obvious glee, a story about her parents' diner during the 1980s. Her family was Liberal, but kept this quiet because their diner was routinely visited by road construction crews. As she told the story, the crew working for the road construction firm whose owners were PC supporters had mistakenly confused their 'Liberal Party diner' with the 'PC Party diner' down the road. Her parents' discretion thus allowed them to enjoy the best of both worlds, reaping partisan-based benefits from supporters of both of the dominant political parties. As well as being humorous, this story reveals something about how deep partisan identity runs in Atlantic Canada.

In the above examples, participants were describing events from their youth, and this prompts the question of whether things have changed for family-owned and -operated businesses since then. In fact, several interviewees had similar situations at the time of the meetings, and their comments were remarkably similar, in that they spoke of avoiding partisan involvement for precisely the same reasons. One woman, who was very much a party insider, squirmed uncomfortably as the discussion turned to her family's retail operation, in spite of the obvious support of her close associates at the meeting:

> I work for my Dad. I haven't shown a lot of interest and involvement in the community. I keep partisanship down. I keep it real quiet. In a small community, you may not want everyone to know. Everybody [here at the meeting] knows that I'm Liberal, been Liberal for generations, but I don't work during campaigns.

This study included a number of participants who operate their own small business, and again, their comments echoed a similar sentiment. An independent insurance broker explained:

> When I do competition for business, there are five people there that are also wanting this business; it's not just me. I don't want any of the ducks that I have in a row not being there because I have been openly political about the wrong party. When I'm doing a presentation up there in front of the whole company, I really don't want them to say, 'She is a staunch Conservative, you know, and we wouldn't like to have our business with that.' And they do do that.

Another insurance broker said that she had thought about running for office – even at the national level – but had hesitated to put more responsibility on her business partner, as it would be impossible to hire anyone to replace her in the firm. I put it directly to her, that perhaps the business could benefit indirectly if she were to act on her political ambitions, by introducing her to a larger network of potential customers and gaining a higher public profile for the firm. She forthrightly rejected this possibility, saying that 'you would lose as many clients as you could gain.' Other interviewees at the meeting concurred with this assessment.

I found these two exchanges particularly surprising because insurance brokers are reputed to be a mainstay of partisan riding associations across Canada. For example, it was their strength at the grassroots that reportedly limited deregulation of the financial services industry in the 1990s and maintain the status quo in which banks were not allowed to sell insurance. Perhaps this apparent disjuncture can be resolved by distinguishing between grassroots participation within the party behind closed doors, on the one hand, and, on the other, the public candidacy that these interviewees shunned.

Small-business operators seek to insulate their enterprises from the partisan fray. Exhibiting an outright partisan preference might bring business from some customers, but at the same time might also expose the business to financial risks. On balance there appears to be a consensus that the risks to the family enterprise outweigh the benefits. But why is such extreme caution required? It is difficult for an urban reader to believe that customers would take their business elsewhere merely because of a difference in voting preference, and the interviewees' comments above do little to explain why. This question will be revisited in the concluding chapter, where interview results from the next chapter will be incorporated to suggest an alternate interpretation of the tension between business owners and their community that goes beyond voting preference.

At the other end of the business spectrum are the large corporations that carry out much of the resource extraction such as mining or pulp and paper processing. Some of these operations are so large and so remote that major corporations built wholly formed towns for their workers' families in relatively recent times – the quintessential company towns. While none of the communities that I visited fit this description, some of the interviewees had lived in such towns earlier in their lives. At one meeting in a mining service centre, several respondents laughed about the sterile artificiality of those young towns, where neighbourhoods were rigidly stratified by the inhabitants' position in the company. They contrasted the general dearth of politics (except, presumably, in regard to employment relations) in those towns with the vibrant political life in their present community, where families had deep roots, and owner-operated mining service companies abounded.

This is not to say that large corporations were absent from all communities in this study. In one town, for example, a pulp mill owned by Abitibi Incorporated had been built nearby, long after the town was established. I asked the participants in this meeting about how Abitibi's presence affected local affairs. My question evoked surprise among the interviewees, some of whom were not even aware who owned the mill:

> People still see the mill as the small-town operation. We don't see what goes on [at head office], and we don't think about it as a multinational corporation. You talk about the mill managers on a first-name basis because they are still your neighbours, and you think of it as the same crowd that has always sat there regardless of who owns it.

Evidently any political dealings that the corporation may undertake do not occur at the local level, but rather through its head office in Montreal. Moreover, few of the women interviewed in this project (or their husbands) were employed by large industrial corporations. Thus, while public life in this town was by no means sterile, companies like Abitibi did not figure large in these women's experience of local public life.

In between the two extremes – small-scale, often family-owned and -operated, businesses and large corporations – are mid-sized locally owned businesses that employ some tens of workers and thus play a significant role in the local economy. Since few of the interviewees in this project were employed in such enterprises, I did not expect them to have much to say about their role in political affairs. This expectation proved to be very wrong. Every single group had a great deal to say about the intersection of politics and mid-sized local businesses. Most such discussions involved indirect effects, in which these businesses were the subject of politics, not actors themselves. This indirect intersection is dealt with separately in the next chapter, because it emerged as an enormously rich topic with significant consequences for women's leadership. Here I limit the discussion to direct effects, in which interviewees perceived electoral results to be influenced by ownership or employment in mid-sized private enterprises.

At one meeting, a participant described a contest in the 1980s for the Conservative Party nomination in her riding, in which she ran against the owner of a local fish-processing plant:

> I didn't know how to get votes [for the nomination]. I didn't know that the way to do it was to go to all the fifty odd polls that there are in [this] county, and offer to do something for those people if they voted for you ... You

know what politics is like ... They [the party members] voted for the man who had promised to employ them in his fish plant.

While it is impossible to verify this rather alarming claim, we shall see in the next chapter that it is consistent with the perceptions of highly qualified women at other meetings.

At a meeting in another province, a veteran campaigner drew on her own campaign experience to assert employer interference in workers' voting behaviour:

> I have knocked on doors for years, and I've had people say, 'I will vote for you but I can't put a sign up because I need to work.' And I've had people call me and say, 'Are you sure they can't tell where I put my X?' That's still at the level it is here. During the last provincial campaign there was one large [private sector] employer in the area who sent out notices when they sent out their monthly statements that had a little chit in it and identified which candidate they were supposed to vote for.

Other members of that group concurred that this case was just one example of a generally prevalent practice. When I asked how an employer could be so high-handed and not worry about how employees would react to such misconduct, the veteran campaigner provided the following interpretation:

> There is a lot of seasonal and short-term employment that people rely on, and the education level for a lot of the people is not high and they're easily intimidated, right? That's the way it was years ago with [fish plant] employees – they weren't asked; they were told how they were to vote. They were allowed to vote but they had to go and vote whatever they were directed to by the office ...There is a lot more of that than you think there is in this area. There are a lot of people so fragile in their assumption that they can't work anywhere else.

When employment is seasonal, short-term, and unskilled, there is little basis to prefer any one employee over another. When employers are able to hire and fire at will, there is perhaps opportunity for partisanship to emerge as a basis for selection. Furthermore, unlike the small businesses discussed above, these larger businesses produce goods and services that are consumed outside the community, so the business owner does not have to be as concerned about local perceptions of the business.

But why was the election result so important to this employer that he would use his power over the employees to support one political party over another? It is difficult to believe that anyone would go to this length to carry out their family's traditional partisan loyalty, especially when it could harm the reputation of the business and potentially offend customers and suppliers. The comments and intonations of the interviewees at the meeting left me with the impression that it made a significant material difference to the future of the business which party won the riding and that the employer saw himself as helping the workers to protect their own jobs. While this particular interviewee felt uncomfortable spelling out exactly how the business would benefit from a particular electoral outcome in this extreme case of employer misconduct, the chapters that follow will offer some clues, as we examine the impact of economic development funding on local businesses, and the ramifications for partisan politics in rural Atlantic Canada, including the effect on women's electoral ambitions.

Summary

The results here suggest that the conventional prohibition against the partisan participation of people employed in the public sector – whether directly as government employees or indirectly as contracted-out service providers – remains an important factor in women's leadership in Atlantic Canada. The public sector employs and/or funds many of the professional women in the region, so any barrier – formal or informal – to their participation in politics can have a strong impact on the recruitment pool of potential candidates for elected office.

Teachers stand out from other public sector workers as an emerging force in women's leadership, particularly in Newfoundland. This pattern was related to the affinity between teaching and politics and to the economic fragility of the communities in question.

In the private sector, interviewees described a nearly universal aversion to partisan politics among small-business owners, based on a fear of offending clients and customers. In spite of the potential benefits that networking within a political party could bring to the business, small-business operators reported seeking to insulate their enterprises from the partisan fray. When viewed alongside the public sector aversion to partisan politics, it is difficult not to infer that rural Atlantic Canadians take their partisan loyalties very seriously indeed.

Conversely, interviewees described a far more vigorous engagement in partisan affairs on the part of mid-sized locally owned businesses that employ substantial numbers of workers, including disturbing allegations of direct intervention in employee voting. These comments gave rise to deeper questions about systemic forces in the rural economies of Atlantic Canada underpinning the relationship between these enterprises and political institutions, which will be addressed in subsequent chapters.

7 The Slushy Intersection between Politics and the Local Economy

One of the strongest common themes to emerge from this study was the respondents' moral aversion to and disapproval of political life as they understood it in their local environment. The two preceding chapters touched on some specific topics that elicited their disapproval, in terms of how politics intersects with their own families and jobs. However, a good deal of the discussions conveyed a more pervasive uneasiness that goes beyond individual-level characteristics, taking the discourse to the level of systemic forces that encompass the entire community. In one group after another, interviewees initiated and carried out intense discussions about how public funds are distributed in their communities and described profound consequences for their own electoral ambitions. By the time I had conducted several meetings, a picture began to emerge, in which much of the disapproval centred on the administration of economic development programs that are aimed at encouraging and providing the infrastructure for the growth of local businesses. Prior to the interviews, the importance of this theme was not anticipated from the literature, nor was its impact on the political participation of the interviewees. It was the flexibility of the interview method employed in this study that allowed and encouraged participants to bring up their own concerns spontaneously. This chapter structures this rather broad, yet centrally important topic, on the basis of the comments contributed by the interviewees, as they grappled with the interactions between the economic and political forces that buffet their communities and that nobody can claim to understand entirely.

The Political Fray

Interviewees at every meeting complained of 'dirty politics' of some sort.

In many cases an interviewee conveyed a generalized distaste rather than a specific complaint. The following comment from a teacher features a tone and attitude that was shared in some regard by women in all of the groups:

> The dirty side of politics are the lies and the manipulation that we have from government. I know that, particularly for decisions about schools, that people were completely manipulated. Everything that I really resent in terms of dirty politics is patronage, where decisions are not being based on what is best economically or what is best for the people. They're being made based on the fact that they went to school together, that they grew up together, or that they worked hard for them in their campaign, or whatever the reasons.

While this comment conveyed an opinion clearly, I found it vague in terms of what specific behaviour was being criticized. This sort of vagueness was common, but not universal, presumably in part because some interviewees were concerned with the consequences of making accusations in a semi-public forum, which included other people from their own community.

A good number of interviewees linked such judgments with a decision to stay out of politics. The following excerpt exemplifies this linkage, while portraying eloquently the interplay among interviewees that was common at these meetings:

> Actually, I have been asked to run both provincially and municipally ... My mom always said, 'Don't become a politician as long as I'm living,' and a more staunch [PC] party supporter than my mother, you'd never find. She didn't want me to lead that kind of life. As for getting people to work on my campaign, if I had to do it, I would do it. I'd get someone else to go ask for money. I guess a lot of it, you feel, when you look at the people we have running for [municipal/county positions].

At this point the economic development officer in the adjacent chair, who was evidently a close friend, leaned over, touched her arm, and whispered with self-conscious laughter, 'Remember the camera.' The first speaker then continued,

> I don't know if I would want to be in that group. I really don't know because I think I would get so frustrated. I really feel badly about what's going on. But I don't know why they think they are the be-all-and-end-all, and I don't

want to put myself in that position, to have to get in there and fight it. I have better things to do. As [another woman] said, I feel I can do more in the community by working with the organizations that I do. I feel that my work in education and health is far more important than sitting behind that council desk, listening to others choose sides, wasting my tax dollars. I love these parties they have – these wonderful planning sessions where they go to [a nearby three-star hotel] on my tax dollar.

The economic development officer then pulled her turtleneck over her mouth, displaying obvious discomfort, and interjected, with a sarcastic tone, in defence of the planning retreats – 'They bond.' (There appeared to me to be an unspoken understanding between the two that the latter had attended the event in question.) To this her friend replied, 'I don't want to put myself in that position of doing what I feel is not right. I'm very comfortable staying at home and doing what I do. I do have family support. My husband says, "Do what you want to do."'

The tone of the cryptic allegations sounded rather sinister. But was there a sound reason for the economic development officer to be squirming uncomfortably? The only substantive allegation in this exchange was that local officials attend planning retreats. To most urban readers this activity must seem quite defensible, particularly considering that the one in question was held at a three-star rural hotel in the same province (and not, say, a five-star hotel in the Caribbean). So why did the economic development officer not muster a better defence? Here it is useful to consider the socioeconomic disparities in the relatively impoverished rural ridings of Atlantic Canada. Elected members are typically well-educated professionals who often enter public life at some personal sacrifice. While their salaries are not competitive with salaries for equivalent positions in the private sector, they are supplemented by generous pensions; and while the overall financial package may not afford a luxurious lifestyle in major urban centres, it certainly affords an affluence that is rare in rural Atlantic Canada. In this environment a weekend at a three-star hotel can appear to some constituents to be an unnecessary extravagance, rather than a minor perquisite to compensate for working on the weekend. A recent national opinion survey on political ethics featured some results that are relevant in this regard. It found that young people and older women preferentially thought that it was unethical for parliamentarians to accept the perquisites that typically accompany executive-level positions. In contrast, middle-aged employed men tended to see no ethical impropriety because, the authors inferred, they were familiar with, and felt themselves entitled to, such perquisites based on their own positions (Mancuso et al. 1998, 112, 118).

In some cases, interviewees made generalizations about differences between how men and women approach politics. A woman who had sought and lost a nomination bid in her provincial riding said:

> Just looking from the outside in, I got close enough to see that it was something I didn't want to do ... It looked like politics was backroom deals, paying off your friends, buying influence where you can get it. If that doesn't work, try threats and intimidation. In that backroom of threats and intimidation, there are some women who cope well in that environment but, for the most part, women don't want any part of that thing. They don't want to be part because they are far too honest and go by settled values that they live their life by. You can't do that if you run for politics. You can't be a good politician if you can't lie and you can't sell out your values.

I was surprised to hear such strongly held perceptions of marginalization at this meeting because, by all appearances, the interviewees are quite privileged women. Some own and operate their own businesses, some hold municipal office, and most are active in the Chamber of Commerce. These are the conventional fishing grounds for political recruitment in Canadian politics.

The foregoing comments illustrate a pervasive feeling of distaste for politics that was shared by a surprisingly high proportion of the interviewees. But they tell us little about what characteristics of local public life are responsible for this consensus. If the political 'fray' is defined as an all-encompassing concept that merges all unpopular policy outcomes, competitive behaviour, and personal connections in a single illegitimate category, its conceptual usefulness is diminished. As the interview series progressed, however, patterns began to emerge among the more specific comments, which, as we shall see, suggest a basis for substantive critiques about how politics are conducted in these communities.

Jobs as Bait

One substantive critique was arrived at in an instructive, albeit circuitous, manner. The discussion began when interviewees made some rather preposterous allegations about electoral fraud in a recent election, based principally on the fact that the deputy returning officer counted the votes in the same house as (and was married to) the campaign manager for the winning candidate. This discussion had a reckless, blustering tone that gave the impression of a vulnerable group bolstering itself against perceived bullying by local elites. The interviewees eventually resolved that electoral irregularities are bound to occur in rural polls simply because there are too few people involved – as scrutineers, poll clerks, and returning officers – to avoid conflict-of-interest situations. Even so, there remained a residual misgiving about the electoral process that the interviewees were then able to isolate:

SPEAKER 1: I don't know about that part, in terms of actually fixing the ballots. But in terms of influencing people to vote in a certain way, yes. When you use jobs as the bait, and you use other things, it's just as bad.
SPEAKER 2: You might as well stuff the ballot boxes. And the bottom line is she's not the only one who is sceptical. Maybe she's the only one who has the balls to say it ...
SPEAKER 3: Watch you don't get shot on the way out of the door.

This critique – 'using jobs as bait ... [is] just as bad' as electoral fraud – refers to a practice known as political patronage. While some participants cited earlier in this chapter used this term in a broad sense to encompass any political decision with which they disagreed, it will be used here in the restricted sense common in the political science literature: 'the giving of employment, grants, contracts and other government perquisites on the basis of partisan affiliation' (Stewart 1994a, 92). Patronage was brought up for criticism, in one form or another, by the participants at every single meeting and more frequently than any other category of disapproved-of behaviour.

Patronage practices were often cited in relation to positions on public works projects such as painting buildings or cutting firewood – jobs for which nearly every able-bodied adult would be qualified. The discussions typically featured harsh moral criticism in terms of nepotism, corruption, and coercion in the electoral process:

I mean, no offence to anybody, but if you had someone that worked at the [public sector site], you were automatically handed a job. If you had someone up there; if you had an in, you had a job [murmured agreement of group].

According to this interviewee, employment at the nearby large public sector installation was a matter of personal connections.

Interviewees at other meetings were able to provide more detailed accounts of the dynamics of patronage in their community and even to connect such hiring practices directly to elected officials. The discussion at one meeting began with the following allegations from a self-described 'rabble-rouser on the left':

[Suppose] for instance, there is a tourist information bureau, and it is run by Joe Bob, so Joe Bob's buddy or his niece or his nephew is going to get the job. So you might not even bother to apply ... Regardless of who is on council, or who is in the political arena, I would have to say from what I have seen thus far, a lot of those jobs that come to the community, they go to families first who are on the council or related to the council or close to them.

When pressed further to be more specific, she said:

Okay, we are talking about [this part of the province], and politically speaking, these are the same people who had been there for years, going up on the same boards, and they seemed to be the people reaping the most rewards from outside influences, because they are in office. They hold office and their families are the ones getting the benefits more so than the average Joe's.

Although this woman had been very active in both partisan and non-partisan organizations, she was relatively new to the community and not well established. At several points in the discussion another participant, who is professionally employed as an economic development officer, corrected the 'rabble-rouser' as to who had been hired from which pot of money, and as to who was an appointed official, and who was professional staff. Significantly, however, the insider professional did not defend the politicians and other officials from accusations of nepotism and favouritism; indeed, she went on to substantiate the accusations herself, as shown in the following discussion, which was sparked by an account of the preceding provincial election campaign:

ECONOMIC DEVELOPMENT OFFICER: And there's jobs to get too if you will have the right ...

SPEAKER 1. And I know it works for sure, when it comes to political parties cause when I ran [labour force development] projects, I got a call from every politician that was in there looking for a job for one of their constituents or a position for one of their constituents. And all I'd say

was there is [an official] route to go through. We'll choose from whoever has their application in. If it is not in at my table by a certain time,
it ain't getting in.

ECONOMIC DEVELOPMENT OFFICER: It goes right to a government member's office. In my situation, the development association is supposed
to be a catalyst, and it administers the money. My story to [a hypothetical person] when she calls looking for a job is, 'We have the authority
to put as many people on [a project] as we can. Whoever has less and
as many weeks gets to go first.' But John Politician is behind me, saying, 'Hire this, this, and this person, and you can't have the money
unless this person comes attached to it,' because it's patronage, political patronage.

RABBLE ROUSER: If you don't give this guy a job, because I'm John Politician and I'm in office right now, then you can kiss your funds for your
Economic Development Association out the door. You can kiss it
goodbye.

ECONOMIC DEVELOPMENT OFFICER: That's exactly how he would present
it.

While these assertions of direct intervention by a sitting elected representative are disturbing, it would be naive to call them wild fabrications,
considering how close the interviewees were to the decision-making process. This account of a politician handing out jobs to supporters after a
successful campaign lends plausibility to another interviewee's claim
(see chapter 6) that she had lost the Conservative Party's nomination to
the owner of a fish plant who had promised jobs to partisan supporters.

As well as telling us something important about the dynamics of public
life in the speakers' community, the conversation excerpted above conveys eloquently where these rural women leaders stand within the local
power structure and about how they relate to each other. These women
are active in civic and partisan affairs, but they are not associated with the
governing party and, hence, are on the margins of political power. In the
course of the conversation, they deferred to the economic development
officer – a quiet, unprepossessing woman – on the basis of her professional experience.

Other women who are closer to the centre of political power described
patronage practices within the governing party with equal distaste. The
following example features a former member of a provincial legislature
and the daughter of another member. In the view of these well-connected and experienced insiders, a patronage appointment would com-
promise their independence and integrity.

SPEAKER 1: Patronage is more biased towards men. I definitely was not 'taken care of,' thanks be to God. In my case I was offered nothing; I went after nothing. The men go after it very, very viciously.

SPEAKER 2: I remember when I worked in Ottawa [as an executive assistant], a guy who was political staff came in and he just took strips off of me (and I was about eighteen years old) because he had been laid off. Because the guy he worked for hadn't been re-elected and he hadn't been taken care of, and this was a man with a family and he blamed me, 'I went to your father [cabinet minister], and I went to this and I went to that, and no one ...' Patronage is not just, 'I think I will give you this job and you that job.' The men go after it viciously; it's absolutely cut-throat.

SPEAKER 1: There is one person who gets a lot of appointments, but he is working the floor every day in there. He gets a lot of plums. In my case, I could work the floor, but how much would it cost me? Personally, I don't want it. If you come to me with it, fine; but that's a different story. But there are so many people in there, being a real pain in the butt they have to do something with them to get them out of their hair. So there is no room for offering people like me anything, and I'm glad. Nobody can ever look at me and say you were looked after.

SPEAKER 2: That's right, [they can't say] you were bought.

In this excerpt, the two women developed an explicitly gendered analysis of government appointments by which men's aggressive pursuit of patronage appointments excludes women who are equally qualified to be appointed. On the principle that 'the squeaky wheel gets the grease,' only those who come to the attention of the powerful people dispensing positions are likely to receive an appointment. Furthermore, these two women saw their non-appointment as proof of their personal integrity.

While a connection between participants' disapproval and their political ambitions was not anticipated, the mere fact that they disapprove is consistent with results of other studies. For example, the Mancuso et al. survey of Canadian public opinion on political ethics found that the entire country is nearly monolithically opposed to a range of perceived ethical violations. If anything, voters in the most stereotypically traditional regions of Quebec and the Atlantic provinces were *less* tolerant of patronage and minor ethical infractions than were people elsewhere. The authors concluded that the 'more critical attitudes in those regions may be due to progressive zeal and a reaction to the deficiencies of the bad old days' (Mancuso et al. 1998, 195). Several other studies have also concluded that routine, large-scale patronage no longer occurs to the same degree as it once did in Atlantic Canada (Young 1986, 133–55; Stewart 1994a; Stewart 1994b; Stewart 2002, 182–3).

Some participants in this study made a point of recognizing this decline in patronage. One, whose personal background makes her opinion particularly credible, spoke of lucrative professional contracts in the distant past:

> If you talk to people a generation above me, like my parents, they talk about the patronage, and will say, 'Are you getting [party] contracts? Is the government giving you business?' Because they feel that I can go in and flash the ancient [party] card and cash goes into my hand and that is very much the way, and my parents, they are in their early sixties, and that is very much the way it worked. It does not work near to that degree now. There are still some contracts that are handed out on a patronage basis but with the Public Tendering Act and the Public Services Commission, there is such a strong reaction to the flamboyant abuse of it before.

At a different meeting, the conversation turned to the toll-gating scandal that occurred under Richard Hatfield's Liberal leadership of the New Brunswick government in the 1970s.[1] One very qualified participant concluded:

> I really hope that we have learned from those experiences and would start to move. But then again, it's rural New Brunswick, and I'll tell you people really think that you should be living and breathing patronage and ... I have a real problem with that because I believe that competence comes above patronage. But it's still very much a learning curve.

When the rest of the group gossiped about examples of so-called dirty politics, this participant corrected them by insisting that 'treating' at election time no longer occurs and that all but the smallest jobs go out for tendering, even at the municipal level, and that campaign finances are handled by the riding executive so as to leave the candidate untainted.

One interviewee suggested that politicians themselves contribute to the perception of greater levels of patronage than actually exist, in order to take political credit for outcomes that were beyond their control:

> And there is a belief. There's people in every community, that we all know that if you have trouble getting whatever pension, go talk to that fellow.

Every community down our end of the county has those people. They think they are political contacts. They're not really because, working on the government side, you know that the person coming in isn't really helping the person to become eligible for anything. They're eligible anyways, but they think that the person helping them has got it for them.

These examples show clearly that the women interviewed in the present study recognize a significant decline in patronage practices, particularly at the high end. Nevertheless, they also made it clear that the issue remains a serious concern and that it has had a real and negative effect on their attitudes towards electoral politics.

One reason for the continued impact of the perception of patronage involves historical continuity. Even if we accept that the worst patronage practices occurred long ago, their legacies can linger stubbornly in communities where families have known each other for generations. At one meeting, some of the younger interviewees proposed that the women there should act collectively to take power from the incompetent politicians that the 'old boys' had set up as their puppets in order to put a stop to local patronage practices in business equipment loans and infrastructure grants for fish-sheds and wharves. Two older women warned them off with a tale from their past:

SPEAKER 1: Not unless you've got a lot of influence and a lot of money going. They're a pretty hard thing to crack, these political parties.
SPEAKER 2: And there are a lot of people still who are concerned about ever speaking up. They never want their vote to be known because of their fear of losing their jobs.
SPEAKER 1: If I'm on an executive of a political party, and it's very strongly intimated that you should vote 'Yeah' for such and such a person because we're handing them this job. Straight out-and-out political patronage. And I'm sitting there and I say, 'No. I don't like this. We said that we were going to quit this political patronage.' So I vote against it. Okay, everything is great. Maybe a year down the line, something comes up and it affects my son or my daughter. They don't hit me in the guts; they go after my family. You're sitting there on that [riding] executive table, and they say, 'You do this; you either do it or' – you do like I did and walk out.
YOUNGER WOMAN: This is what we've got to stop. If you stood up for me, and ended up getting a backlash on that, hopefully [another member of group] would stand up for you. There is no other way to break it

except to cause trouble. You have to put yourself in the hot seat sometimes. I'm always there for you.

SPEAKER 1: I had a daughter who was a single mother with two boys. She
wanted a job as a flagman twenty years ago. She went to the local poll
captain in our area, and she asked him for a job as a flagman, and he
said, 'Go to bed with me and I'll give you the job.' That's how low it
can go.

This story of the single mother and the lecherous poll captain allocating
jobs on a road construction crew is particularly vivid. It suggests that the
mistreatment of the daughter was a form of payback for the earlier event
when the mother (Speaker 1 above) resigned from the riding executive
in anger over political patronage. Two observations come to mind. Most
obviously, it seems ironic that it was the daughter's apparent request for
patronage that opened the door to retribution for the mother's earlier
opposition to patronage. But beyond the allegations being levied, this
conversation is interesting for the light it sheds on the dynamics among
the women themselves. Presumably at one time or another, some lecherous poll captains all across Canada have abused their positions. But
where else would such a story still be told, some twenty years later? In the
stable communities of rural Atlantic Canada this tale retains its currency
as nowhere else. Perhaps, sometimes, history matters too much, and
everyone would be better off forgetting the slights and grievances from a
generation ago. In this context the policy goals advocated by the younger
women at this meeting – gender equity, social inclusion, and empowerment – are like stones skimming across the surface of the ocean, without
affecting the deep currents.

This is not to say that patronage exists only in people's memories.
While it may have declined relative to what it used to be, there is ample
evidence that it remains a thriving practice. The examples provided by
the participants in this study are in agreement with Douglas House's
claim for Newfoundland that small exercises in political patronage are
still the norm. On the basis of his experience in a provincial crown
agency, House reported that 'doing a favour for constituents or loyal
party members is considered by most Newfoundland politicians to be a
normal and acceptable practice, and it is those who refuse to play the
game that are seen as deviant "good-goodies" and holier than thou
(1999, 207).

In addition to conventional patronage practices, there is also evidence
that new forms are constantly evolving. The involvement of a large trans-

national corporation was described. At one meeting, there was heated discussion about Pan-Canadian, which was doing exploratory drilling for offshore oil and gas in the Gulf of St Lawrence. Interviewees related, in credible detail, that Pan-Canadian had made efforts to hire local staff, in cooperation with local economic development authorities. Interviewees had a very definite sense of there being a process by which jobs were allocated to certain towns and then further allocated to individuals on the basis of whose employment insurance benefits were about to expire. Controversy arose because the allocation process had neglected to include one particular town, and because Pan-Canadian had hired a local mayor's wife, even though it was not her 'turn.'

This little local controversy is an example of the politicization of private sector investment. In principle, it seems appropriate that Pan-Canadian should hire local staff in an orderly and fair process, but little attention has been given to how that principle is implemented in practice. There is nothing inherently unethical about such public–private cooperation; in fact, many local residents would consider it insensitive for a major oil exploration company to hire workers at its own discretion, ignoring local conventions about where people stood in the queue of who was next in line for a job. Nonetheless, implementing this hiring process put the economic development authorities up front and centre as the intermediaries between Pan-Canadian and the local population, thus introducing a political element into private sector labour markets.

Newer, modernized, forms of patronage were also reported in the fishing industry. On the basis of her long experience working with the deputy minister in the provincial Department of Fisheries, one woman related that partisan considerations come into play with the allocation of processing licences to fish-plant owners and with the allocation of experimental licences to fish a new species. Experimental licences are not generally publicized, and prospective applicants would usually only know about them if they were notified by a local politician that such licences were about to become available.

Patrons and Clients: Spurning the Service Vocation to Remain above the Fray

At the same time as disapproving of the way in which public sector resources are allocated, many of the women interviewed here expressed an appreciation for the importance of these resources to the economic well-being and future prospects of their communities – and for the role of the elected officials in attracting and overseeing them. The following exchange is a good example of the interplay between these two frames of reference. It begins with a speaker who is professionally and personally immersed in poverty and labour force development issues, explaining why she does not want to pursue elected office or move closer to the electoral process:

SPEAKER 1: A lot of the political things that are of importance [to businessmen and politicians] are not the soft issues or what they call soft issues, [but rather] the economics. So for us it's not what really interests us ... I think it is very good that people get jobs, but I think the infrastructure has to be in place first, so I would want people to be fed, I would want people to be sheltered, I would want to have happy homes. Those would be the things I would want first in my community and I know that that would come from economics and a good economic base, but I don't think you can do one without the other. I think there has to be a balance, and I think when we get around the tables all we hear is 'Oh, we got to create a job for this one, and a job for that one and that fellow over there who has got the ten businesses going, he needs twelve jobs,' and that's why he is sitting at the table. And 95 per cent of the people around the table are there for their own particular interests, because they have financial interests being met at the table.

ECONOMIC-DEVELOPMENT OFFICER: Wait till October – $200,000 will shit in my lap.

SPEAKER 2: That's when the funds come in, and there is a big clamour for money.

ECONOMIC DEVELOPMENT OFFICER: We keep the list of who needs so many hours [of paid labour to qualify for employment insurance benefits], but there's still a bigger list on top of that; these people need to be hired because they helped run a campaign ...

SPEAKER 2: So political motivation is all it is, okay? So economic development officer and her board might decide that this person in the community has a really viable project, but John Politician might come in and say, 'Listen my cousin Bob, he wants to start a goat farm. So you better give him that $100,000.'

ECONOMIC DEVELOPMENT OFFICER: It's not that bad ... [Intervening discussion] ... Family is family, and stuff ... But we have been beaten down [here] for the last four generations, and the major source of income is social services, which is welfare, and besides that there are a few jobs that John's able to create every year which puts a few people on EI [employment insurance benefits]. Hardly any of the population is working steady.

In trying to reconcile these dual strands, it is useful to distinguish the role of a 'patron'[2] from the practice of patronage. The activities of a political patron responsible for dependent clients need not be corrupt, nor even partisan. In fact, carrying out this role can be construed as a moral responsibility. Politicians in many parts of rural Atlantic Canada are not only expected to secure collective wealth for the community by attracting investment; they are expected to attend to the subsistence of individual voters as well, for example, by ensuring that voters receive government support cheques on time or enrolling voters in labour force retraining programs. This understanding of a politician's role was evident in several group discussions. As shown in the following example, there were chuckles of appreciation in response to this description of the previous member of the Legislative Assembly:

SPEAKER 1: John Politician and [his wife] probably did more career placement than Canada Employment.
SPEAKER 2: When you run a campaign in [this county], everybody in this room certainly knows, that even the provincial issues are not what people are voting on, not provincial leaders they're generally voting on, and not [policy] agendas. They are voting on who is going to be at the other end of their telephone. Who is going to get them their fifteen weeks' work? Who is going to see that they get their six months at the government garage? That is the very, very basic issue.

At a different meeting, the women participating knew the local member personally (and his father and his grandfather before him). The text below cannot convey the warm good humour in their voices:

SPEAKER 1: The example I was thinking of, look at how many people end up at John's office after the election to look for jobs.
SPEAKER 2: And John Jr still doles out the jobs too.
SPEAKER 3: I don't see why they bother with an employment office in [town] because they may as well just rely on John's office.
SPEAKER 4: He sure does find a lot of jobs. A lot for young people.

The warmth of these comments was modified, however, when participants proceeded to express disapproval for the specific ways in which the jobs in question were filled:

SPEAKER 5: But John Jr can have the headaches. That guy's phone never stops ringing. Like he is a very close friend of mine, but it would drive me nuts. He's got no private life. I wouldn't want the headaches. In relation to the employment thing, his comment is that people are at his office door, pounding every Monday or whatever. But I have also heard him say, 'Come in. [local manufacturer], for an example, is looking for forty employees.' And there is probably sixty, eighty, a hundred [people] every Monday sitting at his office looking for work, but none of them want that job. Because it doesn't pay enough or whatever. It's full-time; they want term. 'I've made ten dollars an hour at the last job I was at. You don't actually think that I would quit my EI to work for $6.50, with the idea that I could work full-time as opposed to ten weeks here? I would have to be crazy cause I would make more money sitting at home on my EI half the year. So no, I won't take that job.' And it's the same with [another local manufacturer].
SPEAKER 2: See, I think that's where a woman would just say, 'You don't want it, that's it'
SPEAKER 5: They would have to be very, very assertive.
SPEAKER 6: But you have to be able to go to bed at night and be able to sleep.
SPEAKER 4: But if she had that attitude, she would never be voted in again.
SPEAKER 2: I would never be voted in again.

After building a consensus that they would not perpetuate the perceived practice of rounding out seasonal employment with employment insurance benefits, the discussion group proceeded to the following rationale for that position:

SPEAKER 7: The type of arguments that we have at home, now some of them would say, that the fact that John Jr is being hounded by people on EI looking for more work is his father's fault, because that was an idea that he had [that the way to keep] himself elected was to give people jobs.
SPEAKER 5: Just long enough to get their EI.
SPEAKER 7: That's right. And that's the Conservative argument being made, because he didn't benefit people, he kept them here, giving

them work for ten weeks. If he didn't, a lot of our young people might have gone and furthered their education, what have you.

SPEAKER 2: That's the kind of argument [in which] he takes that fifty-two-week job and divides it up between five people. Why not give one person a full-time job?

SPEAKER 8: And you're not dealing with black and white in that situation. The ideal is to have five fifty-two-week jobs with full benefits and four weeks vacation ... But, you know, it's not going to happen.

SPEAKER 5: But it's about keeping five votes as opposed to one.

SPEAKER 2: I'm not thinking of votes though, but long-term economics of the county.

SPEAKER 4: But if you're a politician you have to think of the votes; like it or not, it is always there.

SPEAKER 2: Just long enough to get the government pension. That's it.

In retrospect, the ease with which these women formulated this right-wing critique,[3] and the vociferousness with which they spoke suggests that this critique was commonly held in their circle and well tested in day-to-day discussions. It also demonstrates that these participants' aversion to the political fray is closely associated with a considered rational concern about the net effect on the best interests of the overall community. These women concurred with those in other groups that they would not run (or, if they did, would not be elected) because they would not collude with a system which they saw as hypocritical, dishonest, and manipulative by putting short-term partisan gain (votes) ahead of the community's long-term economic prosperity.

It is important to keep in mind that the practices condemned as immoral by the interviewees in the above discussion are perfectly legal and fall within the scope of public policy. To put them in context of the larger moral spectrum, consider the example of Ralph Payne. In 1994 Mr Payne was sentenced to six months in jail for falsifying employment records at his logging operation in Newfoundland, giving more than a hundred employees credit for work not done, thus allowing them to collect over $1 million in unearned EI benefits. Mr Payne was defiantly unapologetic: 'I'll go to my grave saying that I did nothing wrong.' He added that what he did was no different from federal government make-work projects and that his workers deserved the EI benefits. Perhaps the Liberal Party of Newfoundland agreed with him, as it nominated him as a candidate for the 2003 provincial election. During the election campaign then-Premier Ralph Grimes said he was delighted to have Mr

Payne as a candidate and that 'if [the fraud conviction] is an issue, it's a plus for our candidate because what he did was to help people.' Evidently, the voters felt differently, as Mr Payne was defeated handily by the Conservative incumbent.[4]

In some ways the responsibilities of being a patron in rural Atlantic Canada would seem to be compatible with what has been identified as women's service orientation to politics.[5] Such a service orientation was evident in one interviewee's recollection of her proudest accomplishment as a member of the provincial legislature. A constituent had called for help because her husband had deserted her, leaving her with two small children and no money. She had applied for social assistance, but because her husband had left without a forwarding address and without a separation agreement, and no evidence of desertion, she did not qualify. The interviewee said that she bought bread and bologna for that family, and gave the mother a $20 bill (which was quite a bit of money at the time). The next day, the interviewee arranged to have the woman's application expedited through the Department of Social Services, without further evidence of marital breakdown. The episode touched the politician who was deeply gratified to have been able to help her constituent in a moment of crisis. In her own words, her proudest accomplishment had nothing to do with policy, partisanship, or career advancement, but rather with helping people in need. This example illustrates how the position of being a patron in rural Atlantic Canada meshes well with the traditionally female service orientation to politics.

Yet aspects of this very relationship with the community have been cited by some interviewees as deterrents to participation. At a meeting in a single-industry mining town, three interviewees who are active in civic affairs through a voluntary organization spoke of the futility of trying to serve the community with hopelessly inadequate public funding:

SPEAKER 1: The business of politics in a small town is deciding how to spend your dollars, and you have less dollars every year. You have to make a lot of decisions that will make people unhappy because there is no money for this and no money for that, and I don't think it is something that I would be interested in doing.

SPEAKER 2: You see that was why I tried to run for municipal politics. I was pied off by our town's lack of proactiveness when it came to economic development. They were only interested in maintaining the street lights, maintaining the water and sewer, and maintaining the infrastructure. [It] is a one-industry mining town. The mine put in all this infrastructure like curling clubs and bowling alleys, swimming pools, and whatever, and once the mine shut down, the main thing in the town council was how do we keep all this running, and how do we keep the streets paved. But I didn't see them doing anything proactive to try to build the town. My reason for running was to try to affect the Joe-blow citizen by trying to get the town to be more proactive, in trying to build more from within, or try to bring business in, or whatever it took.

SPEAKER 3: The municipal thing, I think, to get elected you have to make promises, right? Once you get in there, you can't fulfil your promises because the money is not there. You are trying to do the most important things before other things. So that would be a letdown because then you can't do what you promised, and then what happens? Then you have to take a lot of abuse from the public. I don't think I would be willing to take that on.

These speakers imparted a vivid sense of a town in a downward spiral of de-industrialization, in which politicians try to maintain basic municipal infrastructure without the revenues from the private sector to support it. There remains the impression of inhabiting the physical wealth of an earlier industrial era in what may become a ghost town.

Addressing such structural challenges takes a lot more than a twenty-dollar bill and a bologna sandwich. It is no small matter to access the resources required by whole communities in need. This is where the stereotypically masculine traits of a patron arise – competitiveness, ruthlessness, and acquisitiveness. A quip by former Prime Minister Jean Chrétien in 2002 captured this gender stereotype with a vivid, if blunt, metaphor. His Solicitor General Lawrence MacAulay had come under fire for lobbying the RCMP to approve a $3.5 million grant to a group led by Holland College in his province of Prince Edward Island. In response to opposition accusations of conflict of interest over family ties with the college, and comparisons with Chrétien's own lobbying of the Business Development Bank of Canada on behalf of the owner of a hotel in his riding of Shawinigan, Chrétien said, 'Do you want us to be eunuchs in our jobs? We have to do our jobs.'[6] Chrétien's comment is remarkably pithy, and his choice of metaphor speaks volumes. For a politician to be deprived of his ability to channel wealth back to his riding or his province is to be castrated. Chrétien equated being a patron with being a man.

On several occasions I put the question directly to the interviewees: Why couldn't women play the patronage game just as men do? Participants invariably scoffed at the suggestion, expressed abhorrence and moral disapproval of the political fray, and invoked women's essential moral integrity as the explanation. It is important to keep in mind that men have moral scruples too. Professional men working in economic development have also expressed disdain for the politicians who violate rationalized and bureaucratic procedures for partisan gain in their own backyard. For example, Norman Spector, former president of ACOA and deputy minister, wrote a column deploring what he described as partisan grandstanding by former ministers David Dingwall and Lawrence MacAulay. Spector was especially offended that MacAulay insisted that the elected member 'not simply present cheques, but also be the first to inform clients whose projects had been approved by ACOA. ... [MacAulay] wanted our board of directors to understand that politicians, not public servants, would be in charge on his watch.'[7]

As another example, one interviewee described a rather strict moral stance on the part of her husband, a municipal politician who refused to accept campaign donations:

> We decided to run a family campaign. We don't take any donations. We don't owe one person anything. People vote for us because they want to.

I replied that campaign finance is the mother's milk of politics and asked what was wrong with accepting donations. She explained:

> He really doesn't want to owe people, so that he can avoid all this, 'I'll vote for you if you do this and this.' It's maybe getting somebody on a grant or a student job.

Whereas this woman's husband had campaigned successfully on his own dime at the municipal level, it is difficult to imagine how anyone could operate an election campaign at the provincial or national level in this manner. Indeed, the interviewee confirmed that her husband had repeatedly declined to run at the provincial level because of his perception of the expectations that would be incumbent on him in return for accepting political donations.

Disdain for the political fray is widespread among both men and women. Fortunately, the political system does not require that everyone feel comfortable in dealing with the partisan and economic realities of the job; only a relatively small number is required. But those few individuals are crucial. Obviously, there are sufficient numbers of willing men. That the present study found such uniform unwillingness among rural women leaders to embrace the moral ambiguities of being a patron – after seeking out and interviewing individuals of all partisan stripes and levels of responsibility – bodes ill for any imminent increase in the participation of women in electoral politics in Atlantic Canada.

Even those interviewees who had already taken on higher levels of responsibility expressed disillusionment with the service vocation and reluctance to continue. One woman spoke of being cast unwillingly as something of a patron in her job as economic development officer and of feeling particularly overwhelmed by expectations of her at the time of the interview. Surrounded by sympathetic supporters, she explained that she sees her experience as an economic development officer as positioning her for a credible run at public office, but also as a potential threat to her electoral ambitions. She spoke of the particular difficulties that people face in her riding. 'Let's be honest, about 60 per cent of us are on welfare. I mean people are just hanging on.' As a result, people scrutinized the newspaper carefully to see if she had secured a particular application for Human Resources Development Canada funding, and they further scrutinized exactly whom she had hired to work under which HRDC program. The stakes were enormous. Being hired for an HRDC program meant several months of steady work, and several more months of EI benefits; whereas not being hired meant continuing to subsist on social assistance.[8] This woman was building a record of solid expertise in economic development and a high profile in the area, but by the time she would be ready to run for office (a time frame left undefined), she feels she would have made too many enemies, including those whom she had not hired over the years and those who blamed her for grants that she had failed to secure. This woman is at a turning point in her political career. She is disappointed in her ability to establish a more authoritative presence with the old boys in the local party establishment and feels isolated from more progressive elements of the party in the provincial capital. At the same time, she is also a figure of some glamour and repute in the area, who exercises considerable discretion in relation to her dependent 'clients'. While she sympathizes with the efforts of ordinary people to make a living in this part of the world, she also expressed some ambivalence (perhaps verging on resentment) about how much she feels they demand of her. When public sector expenditures are so important to people's livelihoods, it is difficult to avoid disappointing their expectations.

Withdrawal of the Elites

Ironically, while the level of patronage that remains today deters some women from seeking elected office, others are deterred by what they see as an undue backlash against the practice. The preceding section describes how some interviewees have an aversion to taking on the role of patron. Here we find that other interviewees – usually from affluent families – shy away from partisan involvement because they are wary of being cast unfairly as clients, using their political connections to take more than their share from the public trough. We will also see from the comments of other interviewees that their fears of being maligned are well founded.

One woman related that her family owned a heavy equipment firm which carries out construction projects and road work, often through government contracts. She feels that because her family is partisan there is always suspicion that the firm got a public sector contract as a result of patronage. She resents these suspicions because she feels that they skewed the open tendering process (which had been adopted by all governments) *against* her family's firm. She suspects that the government took these perceptions of corruption all too seriously. Her family members sometimes feel that they have to submit ridiculously low bids to get a contract because the government wants to avoid even the appearance of patronage by giving a fair contract to a family known to be active in the local riding association of the governing party. To the agreement of others in the group, she generalized that partisan people are, in effect, penalized for their participation because they must work twice as hard and bend over backwards to avoid the appearance of unfairness. This perceived backlash makes the interviewee think twice about taking on a more public partisan role that would only increase the scrutiny of her and her family and their political connections.

Another small-business owner claimed to have turned down the NDP nomination in her riding for similar reasons:

> Somebody asked me to run for that area, right? And I said no. Because even if you run for some kind of office, I noticed that people got bad-mouthed ... This fella runs for office and he gets a new car and all of a sudden it's because he's ... you know. Even though this guy works hard for a living and has his own career, but because he ran for office, he has this kind of funding coming in or there is a stigma involved as well to running for office. If you gain anything material, even if it's gained by your own work ethic, it's always in the back of somebody's mind in a rural community that said, 'Oh,

yeah, they got funding from the government for that, so they got to build a new house and put a new addition on because now they are on the town council.' Do you know what I'm saying? I'm not saying that it's true. I'm just saying that is the perception.

This woman does not even work in the public sector, but she claimed to worry that what profit her small business produced would become the target of corruption charges should she be elected to office. Hence, she was deterred from seeking the NDP nomination at a very personal level by the possibility of hostile accusations coming her way. In response to these comments, another interviewee in the same group (whose cousin was an elected member of the legislature) said that she would not even buy a new car while serving in public office.

It seems prudent to take these grievances with a grain of salt. After all, these interviewees are rather privileged, and they would stand to benefit from greater acceptance of their position that patronage no longer proliferates and of their perception of an unfair backlash. Fortunately, we do not have to take their word for it. Comments at other meetings supported the existence of such a backlash. On one occasion, a businesswoman squared off against several less well-connected interviewees about the local 'old boys' whom they accused of monopolizing power. An animated, almost combative, exchange began after I asked, 'If the community is in such dire straits, how is it that the old boys manage to make a living?'

SPEAKER 1: Would there have been ACOA money in some of the .... ?
SPEAKER 2: Oh definitely.
SPEAKER 1: The only one I'm thinking who's done a lot of major renovations and growth right now would be Merchant A.
SPEAKER 3: Yeah, there's money there. Also Merchant B said on TV that the Fisheries paid for his cabin.
BUSINESSWOMAN: The money was in the [TAGS] Package.[9] He knew somebody in [branch of ACOA] and said, 'I want some [additional] money to build my cabin.'

Amid exclamations of disgust from others, this woman held her ground in defence of Merchant B.

BUSINESSWOMAN: You could have gotten the money. Yes, you could have. No, you just didn't apply for it.

SPEAKER 4: But [people] didn't know about it, that's the problem.

BUSINESSWOMAN: I did. I was at the meeting. And you [pointing to a different woman] were at the meeting too. When Dave Dingwall [was] there. We all looked down and I – you were there – we went to the meeting. And the guys from government were there.

SPEAKER 2: And they put X amount of dollars in the bank. And I was unemployed, and I didn't have [the minimum funds to qualify]. And that's why Merchant B picked up on it and got it.

BUSINESSWOMAN: It was on the wall that there was a certain amount of money you could get. Merchant C got one; he got some money. And the other one was a big amount of money, which is what Merchant B must have got into.

SPEAKER 2: And there's still money out there.

BUSINESSWOMAN: But it's the risk that you [have to be] willing to take.

SPEAKER 2: We're not in the same boat. I didn't have $5,000 or $6,000 to start out. If I had, it's going to stay in the bank for [my children's] college.

BUSINESSWOMAN: But this is where you make your mistakes. You can't think small, you've got to think big.

SPEAKER 3: You need to have the money in the bank to think big ... I don't think there's a business in [this town] that has expanded in the past ten years and used their own money. Because there's money out there, and they had the connections to go and get it.

These interviewees were surprisingly familiar with the wide range of ACOA funds expended in their local area, without being familiar with the exact eligibility process for receiving those funds. They kept close tabs on which persons received these funds, which seems out of proportion to the actual funds dispersed. The details of the conversation are surprisingly accurate. I confirmed independently that the same Merchant B received a zero-interest loan from ACOA for his project. However, the interviewees' designation of the project as 'his cabin' is perhaps a little misleading, as its official designation is a commercial hunting and fishing lodge. At the level of the official record, it appears that this local businessman was acting in appropriate accordance with the government's objective to promote the tourism industry in the area and that he was assuming some financial risk in carrying out the project. Yet, judging from this conversation, some of the interviewees felt that there was something sleazy in Merchant B's receipt of public sector venture capital for the project. It is impossible to determine whether some hidden favouritism really did play a role in this transaction, but not all of the interviewees concurred in that judgment. In any case, the excerpt above speaks to an overall climate of suspicion that local businesses prosper at public expense because their owners are politically connected to important political insiders. This contributes to a shadow of disrepute over political life that we have seen intimidates some women, in this case business owners, from becoming more involved.

These results suggest a disturbing, albeit extreme, possibility. What would happen if local elites withdrew from partisanship and the institutions of electoral democracy? If this were to come about, it could be argued that the local elites had been betrayed by their governments in Ottawa and the provincial capitals. Could the net effect of trying to purge the system of patronage be to purge community life of partisanship in toto? Donald Savoie observed that the participatory thrust of community economic development is hindered by the lack of administrative capacity, that is, by a shortage of qualified people who are willing to serve on boards and commissions (2000). Consistent with the theme of purging patronage from the system, Savoie excluded the individual politician from any involvement in community economic development. But it can be assumed that the same local elites who are recruited to serve on boards and commissions are the same people who are recruited to join political parties. If, as Savoie claimed, there is a shortage of administrative capacity in one dimension of rural civic life, it seems likely that there is a shortage of capacity in the other dimensions as well.

In the mid-1990s Christopher Lasch proposed the term 'revolt of the elites' to describe the situation in which wealthy Americans had disengaged from local community institutions (1995). While the interviewees in the present project are demonstrably more involved than most people in their communities, both in an economic and civic sense, the net result could be the same. Of course, it is incumbent on political parties in a democracy to strive to resist the iron law of oligarchy by recruiting members from all sectors of society. Nevertheless, a sense of 'we-ness' binding elite patrons to their clients is critical to the collective provision of infrastructure. If local elites were to withdraw from partisanship and civic institutions, questions of class conflict and income redistribution may simply move elsewhere, to perhaps less democratic fora than elections and representative assemblies.

Overall, the discussions with rural women leaders offer a glimpse into a public forum in flux, in which communities are struggling to preserve their electoral system, while purging outdated practices that had 'always' been part and parcel of that system. One effect is that, at least for the time being, negative perceptions of the political fray are viewed by many qualified women as significant deterrents to running for elected office.

Summary

This chapter presents results on one of the strongest themes to emerge from the interviews: participants' moral aversion to and disapproval of political life at the level of the overall community. Some interviewees linked their distaste with politics with a decision to stay out of politics. Others made generalizations that they feel that men are more comfortable with playing dirty politics than women are.

Some of the most well-developed critiques involve patronage practices – the giving of employment, grants, contracts, and other government perquisites on the basis of partisan affiliation. Detailed accounts of partisan-based hiring to fill jobs created by development funds were related by women who straddle the margins of power. Other women who are closer to the centre of political power described patronage practices within the governing party, such as for board appointments, with equal distaste.

Most of the interviewees recognized a significant decline over time in patronage practices, particularly at the high end. Nevertheless, they made it clear that the issue remains a serious concern and has had a real and negative effect on their attitudes towards electoral politics. One reason proposed for its continued impact involves historical continuity, that is, that the legacies of the worst patronage practices linger for generations in close-knit, stable communities. Examples of such intergenerational transmission were encountered in the interviews. In addition to past and ongoing forms of conventional patronage practices, evidence was also found that new forms are constantly evolving.

At the same time as decrying patronage practices as unfair, many interviewees articulated a sophisticated understanding of the distinction between patronage practices and the role of a political patron in Atlantic Canada. While they appreciated the contribution made by politicians who fill the role of a political patron, they nevertheless expressed a uniform unwillingness to embrace the moral ambiguities of doing so themselves. This result from a study that sought out and interviewed rural women leaders of all partisan stripes and levels of responsibility, from church volunteers to former cabinet ministers, bodes ill for any imminent increase in the participation of women in electoral politics in Atlantic Canada.

Ironically, while the remaining level of patronage deters some women from seeking elected office, others are deterred by what they see as an undue backlash against the practice. Some interviewees – usually from affluent families – shy away from partisan involvement because they are wary of being cast unfairly as clients using their political connections to take more than their share from the public trough. A notable exchange between a businesswoman and several other, less-privileged interviewees is presented to illustrate that fears of being maligned are often well founded. This example concerns the distribution of development funds within a particular community. It will be revisited in the next chapter, where it will be referred to as the 'cabin spat.'

8 Structural Contours of Rural Women's Leadership in Atlantic Canada

From a wide variety of partisan perspectives and geographical locations, the rural women leaders interviewed in this study described specific dynamics of public life in their communities that strongly influence their own ambitions and activities. This concluding chapter outlines some of the structural features of rural Atlantic Canada that underlie these dynamics, in an attempt to contextualize and interpret the interview results. This analysis weaves together important findings from each of the preceding chapters, and considers points of comparison and contrast with rural areas elsewhere in Canada. The resulting synthesis illuminates some of the most promising opportunities for and most prohibitive obstacles to increased participation of women in public life, including elected office. Many of the findings bear on the general questions raised in chapter 1 from the point of view of interested stakeholders – governments, non-partisan organizations, and political parties – that wish to increase the numbers of women candidates for elected office. Are there sufficient numbers of potential candidates to supply a substantial increase? Where does one find them? What is the extent and substance of their reluctance to be candidates? What is the extent and substance of local resistance to recruiting more women? At the most basic level, the field work itself gave clear guidance on the first question. That my study was able to go into just about any small town in Atlantic Canada and find several well-educated and well-employed women with substantial experience in public affairs, who could speak at length, and with some authority, about elected office indicates that the numbers are definitely sufficient to supply significant increases beyond the current low levels. But the analytic synthesis below highlights just what a challenge it is to achieve those increases, and surmises to what degree the same obstacles might be present elsewhere in Canada.

Rural Depopulation and Economic Decline

Economic structures in particular loom large in many of the interview results. The economies of rural Atlantic Canada have historically been, and continue to be, dominated by resource extraction industries. Rural manufacturing, especially, has declined precipitously throughout the past century, partly because geographical isolation and poor transportation networks impede access to markets. While resource extraction industries continue to prosper and generate a substantial share of Canada's economic activity, technological innovation has resulted in greatly reduced employment levels over time, thus contributing to a long-term process of urbanization and rural depopulation. Resource extraction industries also produce primarily for export to global markets, whose business cycles can fluctuate unpredictably; thus, profit and production fluctuate accordingly. The economies of most rural areas are dominated by one such industry. This makes them particularly vulnerable to ecological crises, such as the collapse of the cod fishery in the early 1990s. As a result, the rural population that remains is more likely to be employed in the secondary or informal labour force on temporary contracts or to be self-employed in household-based enterprises, operating farms or wood lots. Donald Savoie predicted that 'in future the split between the "haves" and the "less developed" regions will likely be more between urban and rural areas than between Atlantic Canada and Ontario. That is the nature of the new economy' (1997, 50).

A more nuanced approach to the national scene would also include distinctions among rural areas, by considering differences in their specific industrial structures. Savoie's generalization was made near the end of a long commodity bear market that exerted a strain on many resource extraction industries, at the same time that others, such as the cod and salmon fisheries, were devastated by ecological disasters. Hence in the late 1990s, few communities of rural Canada were thriving. However, since that time, some of these industries, such as energy and base metals mining, have rebounded sharply (Coxe 2003), while others, such as farming, fishing, and pulp and paper, have continued to languish. Consequently, some rural communities are experiencing economic booms. For example, Fort St John, British Columbia, saw a surge of investment after a substantial natural gas discovery nearby in 2000 coincided with soaring prices for that commodity. Continued growth in this industry has led to severe local labour shortages (Nikiforuk 2003; Jaremko 2005). At the same time, Prince Rupert, also in British Columbia, whose economy relies heavily on salmon fishing and pulp and paper, has fallen on hard times. The collapse of the fishery and the mill closure in 2001 resulted in a population decrease from 17,000 in the late 1990s to 13,000 in 2004 (Greenwood 2005).

These distinctions are crucial in considering what the results of this study might tell us about women's leadership outside of Atlantic Canada. While some rural communities in Atlantic Canada have benefited from recent changes in the economic cycle, few in the region have had major economic expansions. Some towns, such as Stephenville, Newfoundland, whose economy depends on fishing and pulp, have fallen on hard times, much like Prince Rupert. But for the most part, Atlantic communities have experienced a more gradual decline over recent decades, and so they might be reasonably compared economically with prairie farm communities. As a general rule, Atlantic Canada features less variability from one rural area to another than is the case in other regions (Alasia 1996).

One important consequence for rural women's leadership in Atlantic Canada is that an environment of gradual economic decline and depopulation simultaneously requires and facilitates a high level of civic engagement. As shown in chapter 3, the participants in this project do a great deal of unpaid work for voluntary organizations, as well as a substantial amount of work for nominal pay as appointees on government boards and commissions. Much of this work by the interviewees, and by other experienced and qualified leaders like them, involves strategies to cope with the economic challenges of de-industrialization, while trying to keep existing public infrastructure – libraries, museums, arenas, cemeteries, and so forth – from falling into decay or disuse. At the same time, rural depopulation has contributed to people's willingness to volunteer. Most obviously, with fewer people to carry the load, potential free-riders find it more difficult to shirk their share; thus, civic norms of good neighbourliness are enforced with relative ease via soft coercion. This is not to say that the coercion is unwanted. With relatively few new residents moving in, these communities are characterized by long-standing ties of family and friendship. In this sort of environment, volunteers are often more willing to put substantial efforts into services that benefit all. These considerations help to explain the high level of civic engagement among the women interviewed.

This same analysis helps us to understand why high levels of volunteering were also found in long-standing farm communities in Ontario (Carbert 1995; 2002). We might reasonably infer similar behaviour in some of the older towns in the agricultural belt of southern Manitoba and Saskatchewan. Conversely, we are led to expect quite different patterns of volunteering in a rural boom town. Long-term economic expansions have a major impact on the population structure, as large numbers of young transient workers move in to fill the many job openings. Perhaps the clearest example of a boom-town transformation occurred in Fort McMurray, Alberta, whose population rose from 1,186 in 1961 to over 30,000 in 1981, a twenty-year period in which two major oil sands projects were developed (Fort McMurray Historical Society 1996). As already noted, Fort St John appears to be a good contemporary example of this same pattern. Still considerably smaller than Fort McMurray, it is likely to follow a similar path if current trends continue. A Fort St John city councillor described the period immediately following the natural gas discovery in 2000 as 'the antithesis of stable development beneficial to a community. It was a gold rush mentality' (Nikiforuk 2003, 50). A small town that may be at an earlier stage of this process is Wawa, Ontario, where a promising diamond discovery in 2003 has coupled with a hydro-electric dam project nearby to drive a 'mini-boom,' including a severe housing shortage (Ross 2005). Rapidly expanding, transient, young populations are unlikely to support the same sort of environment of civic expectations and affinity to the community as was found in the long-standing stable communities of Atlantic Canada. In that absence, there would be less overall compulsion to volunteer. For the volunteering that does take place, one might expect a greater focus on activities and goals that serve a more immediate circle of family and friends, and on growing new infrastructure rather than on maintaining existing facilities.

Hence the economic and demographic structures of rural Atlantic Canada have had a positive impact on some aspects of women's leadership, as the pressure to volunteer brings women into public life and provides them with opportunities to build skills and networks. On the face of it, these opportunities should be expected to act as stepping stones to elected office, but clearly, this equation has not operated effectively in rural Atlantic Canada. One reason for this can be found in the toll that voluntary activities take on many women. Comments made during the interviews spoke to a general sense of disarray and apathy in people's lives, as one consequence of the process of depopulation that leaves fewer people to maintain the complete infrastructure of postindustrial life that Canadians expect, even in rural Newfoundland. The conversation excerpt below is a good example:

SPEAKER 1: Maybe we are just tired of looking after others and being in the leadership roles in our community. Maybe we want someone to take care of us for a change.

SPEAKER 2: That's definitely part of it, because you have only so many people who are going to be what you term 'leaders' in anything. And in rural Newfoundland, of course, in smaller communities you have less because they are fewer.

SPEAKER 3: They are all moving away.

SPEAKER 4: If you go to your figure-skating meetings, and your hockey-moms meetings, and your WI meetings, your church meetings, and your basketball meetings, and your grant-committee meetings, you see the same faces, the same core group in your community and by the time you got your couple of kids through the school system, you're exhausted.

An overall sense of collective exhaustion was reported to have pervaded Newfoundland at this time, in which the entire population was finding it difficult to maintain the institutional apparatus of the province. Douglas House characterized Newfoundland in the 1990s in a similar vein saying that, 'people who are now experiencing lost employment and reduced incomes, and who are seeing family members, particularly young people, leave the province in search of work and new opportunities elsewhere are feeling insecure and discouraged about the future for themselves, their families, their communities, and their province. There is a sense of despair that compounds a historic sense of inferiority that still plagues many people,' (1999, 250).

The level of despair described by the interviewees quoted above may seem unwarranted to some readers, who might think of a life of volunteering as idyllic. Part of the interviewees' sense of exhaustion may be related to the 'role-model paradox,' described in chapter 3, in which participants' favourable self-appraisal of their own abilities and activities clashed with their perceptions of being underappreciated by others in their own community. Another component contributing to a sense of exhaustion could be an unspoken fear that their work may come to naught. It is one thing to spend a lifetime working to establish the community infrastructure for grandchildren to enjoy, and it is quite another to preside over the decline of that infrastructure as grandchildren grow up far away, leaving abandoned buildings and a ghost town in the making. In that case high civic engagement is more a matter of making a virtue of necessity than the standard theory of socioeconomic resources admits. These volunteers are reminded daily of the limits of social capital in generating prosperity on the periphery of the North Atlantic.[1] It takes more than civic engagement to bring the mines or the fisheries back into production.

Volunteer burnout helps to explain the failure of high civic engagement to propel women into elected office in rural areas with declining economies and populations, such as in Atlantic Canada. In comparison with other regions, it is interesting to consider how these dynamics might play out in rural areas with rapidly expanding economies and populations. On the one hand, we have found good reason to expect fewer volunteers and less civic engagement overall; on the other, there would be greater opportunities for those who do volunteer to see their efforts meet with success and to come away with a feeling of having accomplished something lasting, worthwhile, and recognized by others. As a concrete example, building a new sports complex to service a growing number of children tends to garner more widespread appreciation than keeping a mouldering museum from closing for another year or two. It is tempting to imagine that the flush of success following such an effort might energize those involved to take on more ambitious projects, including elected office.

Despite the fact that public infrastructure in rural Atlantic Canada is below that found in urban centres, government services continue to play a major role in rural economies, and this too has important implications for women's leadership. Just to maintain minimal Canadian standards in basic services, such as education and health care, requires a proportionately larger presence for the public sector, due to the absence of economies of scale. But that alone cannot account for the concentration that was found here of women leaders in that sector. Chapter 3 shows that over half of the interviewees in this project reported occupations in the public sector, many at the professional level. Evidently, the public sector is particularly important as an employer at the professional level, and especially for women; and evidently their work in that sector sets them up for leadership roles beyond the workplace. This finding helps to provide an initial rough breakdown on the occupational component of the question of where to find potential candidates in rural areas. The preponderance of public sector occupations does not seem to be connected to specific regional characteristics, so we might expect to find a similarly large public sector contingent among women leaders in rural communities throughout Canada, regardless of the industrial structure and economic vitality.

Public sector employment was seen, in chapter 6, to be something of a double-edged sword in regard to women's leadership. The skills, networks, and financial security acquired in these jobs empower women to take on leadership roles. At the same time, these roles are limited by a conventional prohibition against public participation in politics by people employed in the public sector – whether directly as government employees or indirectly as contracted-out service providers. While this prohibition has become less formalized than in the past, the interviews revealed that its remnants continue to deter many of the most qualified women from running for elected office. The ideal of impartiality remains deeply entrenched within the public service. To many government employees taking a public stand on partisan or contested civic issues would feel like a violation of the professional ethos of their workplace. To an even greater degree, public sector entrepreneurs constantly worry about not having contracts renewed, and they are quite aware of the attitudes towards open displays of partisanship within the public service, where those contract decisions are made. Considering how many women in the pool of potential candidates have public sector occupations, the impact of the remaining informal public sector prohibition can hardly be overstated. Creating additional electoral opportunities for this large segment of qualified rural women leaders would require a sea change in the corporate culture of the public service in Atlantic Canada. This, however, is a tall order, given the prohibition's long history and the complex organization and independence of various arms of the public service. While neutrality is obviously essential for public servants who hold specific sensitive positions, there arguably remains a great deal of latitude to encourage freer practices and attitudes among the vast majority of public sector employees and contractors. Looking beyond Atlantic Canada, it remains an outstanding and interesting question whether the public sector prohibition is as strong in other regions.

One bright spot in this otherwise dismal picture is the entry of school teachers into electoral politics. As also discussed in chapter 6, teachers are well positioned through their networks and skills to assume leadership roles, and they are often among the last educated and economically secure to remain in distressed rural areas. Interviewees described a growing influx of teachers into municipal and provincial politics. That women are well represented in the teaching profession suggests that this is a promising route to increased representation in elected office. Since these considerations are not unique to Atlantic Canada, it seems reasonable to expect increasing numbers of rural teachers in politics in other regions as well. One well-known example from Alberta is Deborah Gray, who left the teaching profession to become the first Reform member of Parliament in 1989.

Economic Development and Electoral Democracy

Basic government services are only part of the picture, as governments have always intervened in other sectors of the economy. Prior to the

1980s public policy throughout Canada was directed to large-scale industrial and manufacturing projects. Public investments in the coal mines and steel manufacturing corporations of Cape Breton are familiar examples of this industrial strategy in Atlantic Canada. With large sums of money directed to a small number of ventures, relatively few people were involved in economic development. The policy process was centralized in Ottawa and the provincial capitals, with a few key players from cabinet and the private sector.

The advent of neo-conservatism in the 1980s brought a shift away from nationalization as an industrial strategy throughout the western world. Accordingly, governments across Canada began to privatize public corporations, while pulling back on public sector investment in large-scale industrial ventures.[2] A new appreciation emerged for wealth created through entrepreneurship and small-business formation and for the local context in which a business operates. In contrast to 'hard' industrial development, a new 'soft' approach identified a community's levels of social and human capital as important elements in whether economic development initiatives would succeed (Diochon 2003; House 1999; Savoie 2000). Investment funds were increasingly allocated to a multitude of small players who were dispersed geographically. One net effect has been to democratize the elite networks, as the 'fixers' responsible for the allocation of funds were now further down the pipeline. Another important effect of decentralization has been to make economic development more amenable to the rural focus that emerged. William Milne ended his otherwise buoyantly optimistic appraisal of New Brunswick's future with the proviso that rural parts of the province 'remain very poor compared to [Moncton, Saint John, Fredericton] ... there is need for an aggressive policy to diversify the economies away from the resource-based industries' (1996, 103).[3] These changes brought about the present form of what may be described as the public sector regional economic development industry. In Atlantic Canada this industry is principally funded and administered through the Atlantic Canada Opportunities Agency (ACOA) and Human Resources Development Canada (HRDC) at the federal level, and to a lesser degree, by provincial departments of economic development.

Economic development policy has been subjected to considerable criticism from the right, as have regional variations in employment insurance benefits and equalization payments. It is not unusual for economists to claim that Atlantic Canada is more rural than the rest of Canada precisely as a result of regional development policies that created, or at least perpetuated, the region's traditional way of life. For example, the Atlantic Institute for Market Studies has described rural Atlantic Canada as an artificial product of government intervention seeking to forestall the dominant market-driven processes of urbanization and industrialization (McMahon 2000, 126–43).[4]

Despite these criticisms from the right governments are not about to abandon economic development initiatives in rural areas. So long as regional or rural–urban cleavages continue to exist, there will be a need for governments to facilitate and moderate the bumpy and often painful transitions. In addition to solid economic reasons for addressing such cleavages, Savoie presented a pragmatic consideration: 'Politicians will never buy fully into the neo-conservative agenda. Politicians will wish to intervene and we all have a responsibility to assist them in defining the best possible measures' (1997, 59). We can expect the public sector economic development industry to remain with us for the foreseeable future.

The interview material presented here reveals a profound connection between these government programs and rural women's leadership in Atlantic Canada. In particular, the dynamics of patron–client relations, described in chapter 7, play out under the rubric of this economic development industry. Many of the women interviewed here are well placed to act in the role of patrons, as a result of their prior civic engagement and high standing in the community and their high levels of education and employment, as described in chapter 3. However, some of the most strongly articulated deterrents to electoral aspirations among the interviewees concerned the interaction between politics and the economic-development industry, in its current form. As summarized in chapter 7, interviewees at one meeting after another described, and invariably expressed disdain for, past and ongoing forms of patronage – the giving of employment, grants, contracts, and other government perquisites on the basis of partisan affiliation. A broad consensus emerged among interviewees that they would not make moral concessions to perpetuate what they perceived as an unfair and dysfunctional system.

It is not unusual for ordinary people to distrust politicians or to have disdain for the pursuit of power. But this project did not interview people who were ordinary in regard to politics. The participants were selected according to their demonstrated leadership capacity. The study comprised precisely those women who could plausibly be recruited to stand as candidates for elected office. They all have devoted a good deal of their adult lives to civic activities. Many of them have substantial familiarity with how politics work, and they have developed the experience and networks that could propel them further. Hence a good deal more electoral enthusiasm might reasonably have been expected among this rather elite, hand-picked assortment of leaders. This is not to suggest an essentialist distinction between male and female leaders. Indeed, some men were said to share a similar reluctance. But from a practical point of view, there are clearly sufficient numbers of willing men to fill the required elected positions in rural Atlantic Canada, and this study interviewed a considerable number of women who could conceivably displace some of them. That so few expressed willingness to embrace the moral ambiguities of exercising greater levels of power thus presents a formidable challenge for interested stakeholders who wish to effect significant increases in the numbers of women holding elected office in the region.

Interviewees especially disapproved of direct intervention by elected officials in the allocation of public funds, a practice which was alleged by knowledgeable insiders to occur regularly in some of the communities in which interviews were carried out. A variety of models have been proposed in the literature for the role of a Canadian member of Parliament or provincial legislature in the administration of government initiatives in their ridings. Savoie stated flatly that there is no role, beyond holding the government accountable by asking probing questions (1997, 125). His position is closest to the consensus view of the interviewees. Others are less scrupulous. House reported from Newfoundland that politicians 'wanted to re-assert their control' over the allocation of economic development funds (1999, 193). Allan Gregg proposed that the elected member be 'chief operating officer' for the district, administering and overseeing government policy and programs (2004, 29). David Good, former assistant deputy minister of HRDC, reported that in each Canadian district the local member typically has an informal advisory role to the minister's office on the selection of labour force development projects (2003, 140). Considering that rural election campaigns often hinge on local economic development issues, one could argue that it would be unrealistic to expect the successful candidate to take a completely hands-off approach once elected. This argument would apply both within Atlantic Canada and elsewhere; for example, Sayers described how the 1988 national election campaign featured much more of a local economic focus in rural British Columbia, as compared with Vancouver (1999, 34, 112).

Will the system evolve into a form that the women interviewed could feel more comfortable working within? There is ample evidence that rural Atlantic Canada has already come a long way in reducing discretion in the allocation of public funds. Much of the change occurred when the expenditure of public funds became formally institutionalized in government bureaucracies, especially for universal social programs (Bickerton 1994, 434; Simpson 1988, 32). As shown in chapter 7, the participants in the study recognized the progress but, nevertheless, felt that it had not gone far enough. In fact, their views in 2000 echoed those of James Bickerton, who found that essential elements of the traditional system persisted: 'But in the context of continuing regional economic weakness and dependence, government spending and transfers of all sorts provided the material basis for the continuation of quasi-traditional political regimes, with bureaucratic clientelism and transfer dependency superseding (but not totally displacing) traditional forms of patronage politics. The role of elite networks and political "fixers" did not disappear, nor [did] the importance of patron-client relations' (1994, 445). The political system looks, on the surface of it, much like the nineteenth- century patronage system embedded in the political culture of the region. But Bickerton contended that culture has nothing to do with it. Ottawa reproduces essential elements of the old system through new programs, thereby giving new life to vestiges of the old patron-client system:

> In the Maritimes, parties and political elites have continued to retain a greater semblance of their traditional role of using their influence to acquire resources from the centre to distribute on the periphery, propping up party organizations and cementing political support in the process. And despite, and indeed because of, the modernization of economy and state in the Maritimes, the need for resources from the centre has remained great – a state of affairs that has fostered an inordinate dependence upon the effective use of political mechanisms to win concessions and acquire resources from the centre as a supplement to, or substitute for, market allocations. (1990, 330)

A prime example of supplementing market allocations is presented by an advertisement run in the *Globe and Mail* of 29 August 2002 announcing the sale of a ski resort in Cape Breton. In addition to the attractive physical features of the property, the advertisement assured that 'a business environment rich in government incentives will keep the proponent's investment manageable and mitigate risk.' The wording of this advertisement conveys a concern that potential buyers would find the investment too risky without public sector intervention. In circumstances where the private sector falls short in securing wealth, Bickerton stated that 'politics, *in all its forms*, takes on greater import' (1990, 330).

The stark congruence of assessments, from the differing perspectives of Simpson, Bickerton, and the interviewees in this project, spanning the period 1988 to 2000, suggests that progress in reducing discretion in the allocation of public funds in Atlantic Canada may have approached a plateau. Moreover, the limits of this progress can be traced to rural characteristics that are not confined to any one region. David Siegel outlined obstacles to change that result directly from the structures of governance in sparsely populated areas: 'Small towns are, well, small. Small-town politics and administration are much hands-on processes compared to other jurisdictions. The "hands-on" nature of decision-making means that small-town politicians are more likely to find themselves in situations where they are called upon to make decisions that transparently affect themselves, their families, or their friends (or enemies). This situation personalizes decisions in small towns. When a municipal council is making decisions, it is frequently very clear which individuals and groups will benefit from a decision' (1993, 218–19).[5] It is difficult to see how politics in a rural setting could ever become as formalized as in large cities. There are simply too few people to sit in elected positions, operate the partisan institutions such as riding associations, and administer economic and/or labour force development organizations without overlapping membership or conflicts of interest.

These considerations show that rural communities everywhere share a potential for conflict over patronage. Nevertheless, we cannot infer that rural women's leadership in other regions is uniformly inhibited by an unwillingness to embrace the moral ambiguities of being a patron, as has been found for the Atlantic region. To be sure, patronage practices abound everywhere, and they are particularly noticeable in small towns. But this does not mean that local politics are always best understood in those terms. One needs to ask the question: How much importance is attached to local patronage practices? Bickerton's analysis above suggests that part of the answer to this question lies in how dominant a role the public sector plays in the local economy. Not all rural areas are poor, and not all poor rural areas receive the same level of public support. As noted above, regions outside Atlantic Canada feature greater variability in these respects, from one rural area to another. In more prosperous towns with thriving private sector economies, public sector transfers and expenditures typically form a proportionally smaller component of the economy than is the case in most areas of rural Atlantic Canada. Hence there is less scope for a politician to assume the role of a patron of dependent clients. Even though individual politicians do dispense patronage, just like their counterparts in the Atlantic region, the dollars at their disposal make less of a splash, when measured against more afflu-ent living standards and the relatively larger pool of private sector eco-nomic activity. A rural woman leader considering candidacy in Fort St John would not likely face as dire a dilemma as that described by Atlantic interviewees (chapter 7), in which they saw a politician trading away the community's long-term economic prospects in exchange for votes, by providing as many seasonal jobs as possible. Neither would she likely experience the same level of discomfort that interviewees expressed about a planning retreat at a nearby hotel that was perceived to be extravagant, relative to local living standards.

Patron-client relations might be expected to be more prevalent in less prosperous areas. But other factors besides overall wealth need to be considered as well. For example, Melfort, Saskatchewan, a relatively sta-ble agricultural service centre, might be compared in some respects with many towns in Atlantic Canada. The average income is below the provin-cial average, and substantially below the national average, and includes a relatively high proportion that comes from government transfers.[6] How-ever, one cannot infer equivalent patron-client relations from these numbers alone. Measures of income from government transfers include a number of different sources, and the role of local politicians in secur-ing those transfers varies considerably. Lower unemployment levels limit the incentive and opportunity for a politician to engage in a practice that was criticized by numerous interviewees in Atlantic Canada: arranging short-term employment sufficient for constituents to secure employment insurance eligibility. Furthermore, EI eligibility requirements are more stringent in Saskatchewan than in Atlantic Canada. Regional differences in the level of economic development funding also affect how much dis-cretionary influence a politician holds over the local economy. Thus, while people throughout Canada share in the moral disapproval of patronage practices that was found in Atlantic Canada (Mancuso et al. 1998), the extent to which this disapproval acts as a barrier to rural women's leadership in other regions likely varies a great deal, depending on specific local circumstances, especially economic vitality and, to a lesser extent, regional variations in the public policy regime.

Realistically, some women will always be deterred by the moral ambi-guities of administering public resources under such intimate circum-stances. But there is, of course, a distribution of attitudes, even where this barrier is relatively pervasive, as in Atlantic Canada. It seems likely that there is room for enough change to suit some qualified women. The results presented here suggest that a more tightly regulated system with a bit more distance between the decision-making process and the affected constituents would offer more electoral opportunities for women.

It is possible that the degree of expansion and formalization that has occurred to date in the economic development industry has already had a modest impact in helping a few women to get their foot in the door. The present discussion series includes a number of women professionally employed in the economic development industry, mostly as permanent staff working for municipal-level boards. These women have acquired positions of some responsibility that were not available until recently. The growth and decentralization of this industry established economic development professionals as important players in civic life by the end of the 1990s. Economic developers oversee a panoply of overlapping programs emanating chiefly from Ottawa (through ACOA) and, to a lesser extent, from the provincial capital. They are the people in the field implementing the development agendas designed at the centre (House 1999, 192).

In addition to their access to funds, the professional staff working in economic development are important individuals because they acquire a range of networks and contacts that are beyond the reach of most people. Economic developers operate at a crucial nexus among government, business, and the public at large, as few other officials do. To be sure, governments employ field officers throughout rural Canada – in fish and wildlife protection, motor vehicles licensing, and so on – but these staff operate under restricted job descriptions, with very limited mandates. In contrast, economic developers are employed to seek out and create new, far-sighted opportunities for the collective good. Their networks are all the more valuable, as it became apparent while arranging the interviews that the major political parties have largely failed to establish rural-urban contacts for women in all four Atlantic provinces.[7]

In the interviews examined in this book, economic development professionals consistently stood out as sophisticated and knowledgeable insiders. Their insightful contributions are highlighted throughout chapters 5, 6, and 7. As relatively privileged women, they are not the designated clientele for recent initiatives to promote women's empowerment as part of the policy shift to the development of a community's soft human and social capital, but they certainly seem to be empowered by the industry. Their detailed knowledge of local affairs typically exceeded that of party insiders at the table, including women who had run as candidates or who had been invited to run and declined. The sophistication of these economic development professionals can be related to their positions at Sharon Sutherland's (2001) slushy intersection of politics and policy. One implication is that these women are particularly well qualified to stand as candidates for public office, both in Atlantic Canada and elsewhere.[8] Moreover, their experience does not slot them into any one political party, as they administer programs that contain what could be construed as both right-wing and left-wing elements.

This study has found that, so far, even these most qualified women share much of the same disillusionment with public life as the other rural women leaders in Atlantic Canada. Economic development professionals spoke of the long-term damage to the economy wrought by a jobs-for-votes environment aimed at satisfying the short-term needs of distressed individuals. There may have been a touch of snobbery behind some of the comments expressing disdain for having to deal with some people who were described as constantly clamouring for their share of available funds. But, to be fair, part of the disapproval stems from a reasoned judgment that making an allocation based on whether it is someone's 'turn' takes away from the more important goal to generate a long-term economic benefit for all. Hence we have the paradox that the advent of the economic development industry has created a cadre of specially qualified rural women leaders and helped them to get their foot in the door of electoral politics; yet their experience in that same industry has made them reluctant to walk through that door. On the bright side, any efforts to clean up the political interface could be expected to have a particularly favourable impact on these most likely potential candidates.

Class Tensions

In addition to concern for the future of the overall community, some interviewees were deterred from partisan politics by a personal fear of being maligned by others as corrupt recipients of government largesse. In most cases these were wealthier women whose families operate sizable local businesses. A good example of the maligning that they feared is presented by the 'cabin spat' over public sector financing of local businesses, including a merchant's lodge (as described in chapter 7). While not all those in the discussion had a clear sense of how the program worked, they had no trouble keeping tabs on whom among their neighbours was receiving what ACOA money from which pot, and how it was being spent – and all for such relatively small sums of money. Although the interviewees did not disclose the precise amounts of the loans, their discussion made it clear that they were roughly on the order of $10,000. (This scale was later found to be consistent with the typical interest-free loan account reported in the annual report for that year by the corresponding branch of ACOA.) It seems that even relatively small amounts of public sector funds can have enormous rippling influence that is entirely out of proportion to the actual amount expended. In this case, the conjunction of transparency and wariness about the distribution of public funds resulted in a generalized distrust of the political system by those not directly involved.

One of the features of this 'cabin spat' reproduces closely the principal finding of a study commissioned by ACOA, during this same period, to investigate public perceptions of the agency (Corporate Research Associates 2002). That study reported that government officials and business people who had established a working relationship with ACOA had a positive impression and thought well of the agency. Members of the general population (excluding government employees, educators, and small-business owners) had little knowledge of ACOA's operations or achievements, but still, they thought poorly of the agency based on negative stories in the media. Furthermore, 'virtually all participants [in the general population] consider ACOA to be politically motivated. Those who are fortunate enough to receive assistance from ACOA were seen as having some sort of political connection which made their accessing resources much easier' (2002, 37). These findings indicate a class dimension to tensions over government funding. In the cabin spat among interviewees, it was the lone business owner who defended the fairness and general accessibility of the program, while the sceptics could be described as less elite and not as close to the process. It might be tempting for government to surmise from the ACOA report described above that only public perceptions need to be addressed, and not the administration of the funding programs. That may be a dangerous approach. Continued conflict over these issues is destructive to rural communities, and it spills over into every aspect of public life, including, as was found here, women's leadership.

Recognizing this tension helps us to understand one of the more puzzling results of chapter 6: business owners worried that they would lose customers if they showed their partisan stripes. It is difficult to believe that customers would take their business elsewhere merely because the owner of the business voted for a different party. It is far more plausible that a business owner would fear that customers would perceive the business as 'eating at the public trough' as a result of its partisan ties. Clearly, a general suspicion of sleaze would threaten the viability of a business whose customer base is fixed. Since the public sector plays such a large role in the rural economy, it is inevitable that most businesses would have dealings with the public sector. When any such transaction – even as mundane as a snow-plowing contract – is viewed by some as corrupt, we can see how important it is for business owners to keep as quiet as possible about their partisanship and about their dealings with the public sector economy.

Chapter 7 describes a woman whose family members did not keep quiet and paid a price for their openness. She expressed pride in their partisan involvement, which she saw as carrying out their civic duties. While this particular woman felt compelled to assert what she saw as her rights and responsibilities, she recognized that this strategy brought her and her family into conflict with others in the community. She also felt that displaying their partisanship made it harder, not easier, to get government contracts, because in her view responsible officials bend over backwards to avoid the appearance of favouritism.

It is understandable that other rural women in similar circumstances have chosen a course of conflict avoidance by not becoming active in partisan politics and taking care to be far more discreet about their preferences. It may not be possible to keep the award of government contracts secret in a small community, but it is feasible to keep a low profile by not getting visibly involved in electoral politics in the first place. This reinterpretation of the results from chapter 6 is summed up well by one of the interviewees: 'If the contract is awarded to my family's firm, it's not [perceived to be] an honest contract if people know the family is Liberal. They're basically going to drive to the next town to do their business.'

The finding that many rural women leaders are reluctant to seek elected office should not be taken to imply that the job is theirs for the taking. The status and desirability of elected office are also relevant here. Men have historically dominated positions of prestige and responsibility in most fields of endeavour, and this tendency persists to varying degrees. In politics it has become a truism that the relative importance of an elected office determines (inversely) the likelihood of it being held by a woman. This tendency is often summarized in terms of a familiar rule about women in electoral politics: 'the higher, the fewer' (Bashevkin 1985, 53). The presumption behind this characterization is that higher levels of office hold more power and prestige. At first glance, this rule might seem at odds with the low proportions of women elected in rural districts in Atlantic Canada. These ridings are not particularly powerful ridings at either the provincial or national levels. Naive application of 'the higher, the fewer' would lead us to expect greater numbers of women to be elected there, especially if they did not hold a cabinet position.[9]

But that expectation ignores the local context for politicians within their own electoral districts. Bickerton's analysis of how important politics are in economically distressed areas is consistent with the present interviews in this regard. To constituents in rural Atlantic Canada, their elected representatives hold positions of considerable power and prestige, by virtue of their influence over a substantial proportion of the overall local economy, as well as their *relatively* high salaries. Of course, urban MPs and MLAs earn the same salaries, and the local economies in their ridings are often just as reliant on public sector expenditures. However, those salaries are less impressive when compared with urban salaries, particularly at the professional level. In addition, the representative of an urban district is usually perceived to have relatively less influence over the size and allocation of public expenditures there.[10] In the present context, it might make more sense to restate the rule more precisely as 'the higher the status within the local environment, the fewer.' The high status of the job of a rural politician in Atlantic Canada helps to contextualize the vicious nomination battles and dirty tactics described by some interviewees who had stood for nomination or election. In this light, one cannot entirely dismiss the possibility that for some rural women leaders, a disavowal of electoral ambition is, in part, a reaction to the futility of earlier, thwarted, ambition – sour grapes, in effect.

Application of this rule to other regions of Canada should recognize the variability that characterizes those regions. In most prairie farm towns the salary of an MLA or MP would be just as prestigious as in a typical rural Atlantic town; less so in more prosperous farm communities in southern Ontario, and even less in a rapidly expanding resource town with a thriving private sector economy. Similar patterns hold outside Canada as well. Based on their work on the dearth of women in southern U.S. state legislatures, David Lublin and Sarah Brewer came to their own version of the restated rule above: 'Women are most likely to win public offices in areas where men do not want the jobs' (2003, 391).[11]

Collective Dynamics Maintaining the Status Quo

Personal ambition and enthusiasm are only part of the story. Other people's influence and expectations play a major role as well, and especially so for female recruits. Lynda Erickson's survey of candidates in the 1993 Canadian national election found that women candidates were almost twice as likely to report having been contacted (and presumably encouraged) by both local and outside party officials. On this basis, she concluded that 'women may require more organizational support in order to participate effectively in national politics' (1998, 247). Rural women likely need even more support than the predominantly urban candidates in Erickson's study, given their geographical isolation, their history of exclusion, and their pervasive reluctance.

An example was presented in chapter 5 of a politician's reluctant son who was pressured by family and party insiders, including the premier, to assume his father's seat, and who subsequently went on to play a prominent political role in the region. Why was he promoted over a keener female competitor who was regarded as very capable? And why are other rural Atlantic women not being recruited more often and more vigorously than has been the case to date? This story echoes David Niven's study of state-legislative candidates in the United States, which found that local party officials consistently and significantly favoured prospective recruits who were most like themselves in terms of occupations and personality traits. Since most senior party officials were men, they were, in effect, biased against prospective female candidates (1998, 124).

But framing this bias as an abstract, possibly irrational, psychological state would do little to explain why rural areas have particularly low rates of female candidacy. Moreover, a hypothesis of pure sexism flies in the face of opinion polls, not to mention unbiased voter behaviour. The interviews presented here provide clues to a more nuanced interpretation based on rational motivations. They highlighted several factors that can be linked to weak communal support for women's candidacy and revealed a pervasive collective dynamics behind what are sometimes described as traditional political practices. While few instances of overt sexism were encountered, as we will see, these practices serve to maintain an environment that is resistant to change.

In chapter 5 interviewees discuss partisan politics in terms that seem ritualized to an urban observer. They described a convention by which preference is given to recruiting candidates for elected office from particular families that had produced politicians in previous generations. In one important case this practice was specifically linked to the anticipation of a tight election. The reasoning seemed to be that supporters of the political party in question had reached an earlier consensus on this person's father and so would see the son's candidacy as an easy means to maintain that consensus. All this presupposes that consensus within the party is highly valued in this district. In the end that party's strategy was successful in that election. While it would be naive to claim that the voters did not consider the merits of all the candidates, there is no doubt that the family legacy of the winner played a significant role in the overall result.

Deference to leading families can be a convenient way to avoid open feuds arising from excessive competition within parties. It can also help to maintain a consistent flow of jobs and development funds, if those leading families can be counted on to draw on their experience and political networks to that end. Conventions that facilitate consensus can thus help to achieve important shared objectives. According to Savoie, 'in areas of economic distress ... there is an urgent need to focus energy and resources on designing and building local organizations and institutions and on finding ways to generate new economic activities. The effect of intercommunity rivalries is to consume energy precisely at the wrong time, in the wrong place, and on the wrong issues' (2000, 119). Sharing high regard for established family names among electoral candidates can be viewed as a strategy to avoid such destructive rivalries. This sort of collective behaviour does not require each individual to calculate costs and benefits. In fact, it is all the more powerful to the extent that it is incorporated into the social and political conventions and attitudes that shape the environment in which people grow up.

These conventions can only be developed under the conditions of multigenerational population stability that is so common in rural communities in Atlantic Canada. Conversely, in a commodity boom town featuring rapid population growth and high transience, many people will have arrived only recently, and many live far from their extended families. Hence, there would be less opportunity for leading families to be established and to maintain their prestige within the public life of newer and less stable communities.

Besides the leading political families, other families in rural Atlantic Canada have collective identities as well. The idea of living up to, and not disgracing, their own family's name weighed heavily on a number of interviewees' electoral ambitions. It is a tribute to the power of community expectations that interviewees' fears about how their candidacy might impact the reputation or business of aging parents were the predominant family-based concerns. By contrast, interviewees were not particularly deterred by difficulties in balancing their family responsibilities to husbands and children with their civic activities. This counterintuitive result emerged only when the extended interviews moved past the initial universal script of gender-role constraints in the abstract and delved into individual women's concrete personal experience. It suggests that measures by governments or political parties to help women candidates fulfil their domestic obligations, such as provision of child care, would have little impact on rural women's candidacy.

The family vote is another ritualized convention that can only arise in stable communities. In chapter 5 interviewees discuss the expectation that whole families will vote the same way. While this convention is often broken by individual family members, especially those who are politically sophisticated, there appeared to be a lingering stigma, and some guilt, attached to that choice – a sense of being provocative by not going with the flow. The family vote can definitely be seen as another mechanism to ritualize partisanship and avoid excessive competition. Remnants of the family vote may help to explain two puzzling results from chapter 3 regarding interviewee partisanship. First, friends and associates attending the same meetings did not tend to share the same partisan identity; and second, the partisan identity of interviewees was not strongly associated with their ideological view on the trade-off between taxes and social programs. Perhaps some of the interviewees were voting according to their family tradition, rather than according to their opinions that they shared with their current circle of friends.

Participants' views on images of leadership (chapter 4) also conveyed similar conventions and attitudes. On the one hand, they knew the universal style code for what a successful female politician should look like and what sort of visual nuances fit with which political party. These preferences were not distinct from urban sensibilities. On the other hand, most participants felt compelled to express discomfort with voicing these judgments and disapproval of the whole idea that appearance should matter at all. Their comments suggest that emphasis on image feels too manipulative and superficially competitive for their taste. This attitude meshes well with a consensual approach to choosing candidates.

This same attitude came to light when participants were asked to discuss women who had become well-known politicians. Some related what can only be described as cautionary tales centring around humiliation in front of family and friends or, alternatively, conflict with family and friends. Even experiences that could well be interpreted as success stories – such as Jane Stewart, who served in cabinet at the national level – were often framed instead as failures. These comments suggest that, for some of the interviewees, the emergence of conflict itself constitutes failure.

The net effect of all of these social and political conventions is that they contribute to a pervasive tendency for rural communities in Atlantic Canada to maintain the political status quo. Even when there is no deep-seated prejudice against an alternative choice of candidate, it is usually more prudent for a party, or the voters, to go with the more familiar choice – someone with well-established networks and connections. In this environment, any change, however small, is a potential risk, and a potential source of conflict. The tendency to inertia is not strong enough to propel a criminal or incompetent candidate into office; rather, it is just enough to tip the balance in close races and to deter serious challengers from entering a race. Its pervasiveness translates into the high incumbency rates that are known to characterize politics in Atlantic Canada (Stewart 2002). These same considerations also go a long way to understanding the NDP's limited electoral success to date in the region, outside of major centres.[12] While high incumbency and adherence to a two-party system may sometimes benefit individual communities, both of these characteristics diminish the quality of democracy.

Part of this diminishment is a lower probability of women being nominated and elected. A purely statistical linkage to women holding elected office has been documented elsewhere using mathematical models in which these same characteristics – incumbency rates and NDP success – were input as independent variables (e.g., Matland and Studlar 1998). The discussions here with rural women leaders put flesh on the bones of these mathematical models by revealing that these seemingly simple measurable characteristics are, in fact, only particular end results of a myriad of economic, political, and social dynamics that play out locally among people who interact with each other on all of these levels simultaneously. It is true that high incumbency rates correlate to low numbers of women elected, but that does not itself constitute an explanation. A high incumbency rate is not an embedded characteristic of a district or its political culture, but rather a reasoned collective strategy, responding to the current political realities of living in a fragile and poorly diversified economy.

The contributions to public life of rural women leaders outside elected office – as economic development officers, government board appointees, public sector entrepreneurs, and community volunteers – are crucial, as policymakers at the centre fret about a crisis of administrative capacity in rural areas. Several interviewees claimed that their non-elected positions afford greater opportunity to bring about positive change than would elected office. Nevertheless, the election of women does matter, and the quality of democracy would be improved if more women found their way to public office.

It is well established that the low numbers of women elected throughout Canada (as well as the United States) are largely attributable to low candidacy levels. Much of the discussion in the literature has centred on whether external barriers act to prevent women from running or whether women are simply reluctant to run. Prior studies have often emphasized one explanation over the other. This book reports that both categories of effects are important in rural Atlantic Canada. Moreover, it moves beyond assigning blame, by exploring the motivations behind the barriers and behind the reluctance. There are reasoned positions underpinning the behaviour of important actors on both sides. Their motivations are deeper than individual characteristics such as gender-based prejudice on the part of gatekeepers or the fear of losing on the part of reluctant potential candidates.

The tendency of rural communities to maintain the status quo has been linked to collective strategies tailored to the economic and political environment that has prevailed in rural Atlantic Canada for some decades. The immediacy of the need to nurture fragile economies magnifies the importance of the precise relationship between political representatives and government and attaches a tangible risk to the idea of change, even seemingly minor change, and especially change for the sake of change. The reluctance of women to stand for elected office has also been situated in this environment. We have seen that this reluctance is less about husbands and children, and more about parents and in-laws, and their standing and reputation in the community, than has previously been imagined; less about traditional gender roles and more about job security and the continued vitality of family businesses. The heightened importance of politics, and the fragility of economic life, combine to present a tangible risk to putting one's name forward, especially if it is for the wrong political party or faction. The interviews also revealed that quite a few women, particularly those who have worked closely with politicians, share a reasoned reluctance based on an informed disdain for what they see as questionable political practices and a dysfunctional relationship between politicians and the electorate. Many have turned up their noses at the idea of running for elected office in a system of which they disapprove, in which they see short-term interests of a few being traded against long-term community viability. The very fact that all of these impediments to women's election can be formulated rationally, and related to entrenched political and economic conditions, makes the prospect of bringing about positive change all the more challenging.

In the course of describing their own experiences and ambitions, interviewees told a great deal about their surrounding environment. Their detailed comments, taken together, lead inexorably to a description of public life in terms of the vital structures that sustain individuals and communities. Here, politics are simply too important to be confined to a separate sphere of life. To these women, power is exercised at the intersections between politics and their family, between politics and their occupations, and between politics and the overall local economy. In providing their vivid and intimate description of these confluences, from their own points of view and based on their own experiences, the participants in this project have enriched our understanding of the full spectrum of public life in Atlantic Canada, including the nature of, and future prospects for, rural women's leadership.

Notes

1 Introduction

1 This calculation includes 39 urban and suburban ridings forming a geographically contiguous block of high population density electoral districts
   running from Scarborough in the east through Mississauga, Oakville, Burl-
   ington, and Hamilton in the west, and from Lake Ontario in the south to
   Richmond Hill in the north. The result (14/39 = 36 per cent) is not very sensitive to where one draws the line on the surrounding urban area; the proportion of Toronto-area seats held by women ranges from 32 to 40 per cent,
   depending on which ridings are included. Election results were obtained
   from Elections Canada.
2 This calculation includes 34 urban and suburban ridings forming a geographically contiguous block of high population density electoral districts on
   and around the island of Montreal. The result (13/34 = 38 per cent) is not
   very sensitive to where one draws the line on the surrounding urban area;
   the proportion of Montreal-area seats held by women ranges from 36 to 40
   per cent, depending on which ridings are included. Election results were
   obtained from Elections Canada.
3 If we exclude the 39 Toronto and surrounding area ridings used in the earlier calculation, we find that the 'rest-of-Ontario' proportion drops to only
   19 per cent, which is near or below the national average. Similarly, the 'rest-
   of-Quebec' proportion of federal seats held by women is only 17 per cent.
   And these lower proportions include other urban centres, such as Ottawa-
   Gatineau and the city of Quebec, so they should not be construed as rural
   proportions.
4 District populations and areas were obtained from Elections Canada website.
   The median population density among Ontario federal ridings is close to

900 people per square kilometre, which is equivalent to about one acre for a family of four. In agreement with the appearance of the electoral map, most of the sparser half of the ridings are far sparser than the median; fully 40 of the 53 ridings in the more rural half have population densities below 100 people per square kilometre, which is equivalent to one hectare (10,000 square metres) for each person.

5 The remaining three Ontario seats in the more rural half of the list were won by NDP men.

6 In the more urban Ontario ridings, where Liberal support was much stronger, that party nominated far more female candidates (21 of 53, or 40 per cent). Consequently, far more of the Liberal urban ridings were won by women (19 of 47, also 40 per cent). The high success rate of female Liberal candidates in these more-urban ridings (19 winners from among 21 candidates) was closely matched by male Liberal candidates (28 winners from among 32 candidates).

7 This calculation includes candidates who won at least half as many votes as the winner in the district; the result is not sensitive to changes in the criterion.

8 Burrell 1994; Glaser 1996; Lublin and Brewer 2003; MacManus et al. 1998.

9 The provincial aggregate shown is calculated by assigning equal weight to all seats in provincial legislatures in the ten Canadian provinces.

10 The Reform Party was the predecessor to the Canadian Alliance, which merged with the Progressive Conservative Party in 2003 to create the Conservative Party of Canada. It was founded in 1987 as a grassroots right-wing protest party in western Canada.

11 The election of women has emerged as a critical building block of legitimacy in fledgling democracies around the world. For example, Isobel Coleman of the U.S. Council on Foreign Relations wrote, 'women need to be nurtured, both as candidates and voters, particularly in ... countries where their role in political and civil society has long been repressed' (2003, 11).

A renowned prototype is the U.S. military occupation of postwar Japan. General MacArthur and his staff thought that promoting women's equality rights, including candidacy for elected office, would prevent Japan from reverting to fascism or going to war again, and so they brought in prewar suffragists to campaign for women's equal rights. Japan's prewar suffrage movement had established international ties; the most famous of Japanese political women, Ichikawa Fusae, lived in the United States from 1920 to 1924, where she was in contact with such American suffragists as Carrie Chapman Catt and Alice Paul (see Pharr 1981, 19). The prewar suffrage movement had never built a mass base of support and had effectively disappeared under Japanese fascism in the 1930s and 1940s. Its remnants were incorporated into the Allied agenda: 'To the extent that women's demands were perceived to be consistent with the goals of the Supreme Command for the Allied Powers administration, there was an official willingness to consult and cooperate with key proponents of women's rights' (Buckley 1994, 151). Rather than seeing Japanese women as passive objects of Allied policy, Susan Pharr implied that there was outright collusion between Occupation officials and a few elite women: 'In a period when Japan's own leadership was discredited and in disarray and when overt resistance to occupation policy was impossible, the occupation in Japan functioned much like a revolutionary council following a highly successful military coup in support of a far-reaching program of social change' (1981, 29).

Since then, the election of women has become an explicit goal sought in the course of building representative institutions under new regimes. For example, on the eve of the overthrow of the Taliban regime in Afghanistan, Sameena Nazir-Ford, senior research coordinator for Freedom House, wrote, 'Afghan women leaders ... have the skills needed to build the pillars of a peaceful and plural society ... Excluding Afghan women from the process is not only unfair, it undermines the chances for a sustainable peace' (cited in Groves 2001, 759).

12 Atlantic Canada comprises the provinces of New Brunswick, Prince Edward Island, Nova Scotia, and Newfoundland and Labrador.

13 The seven unambiguously urban federal ridings in Atlantic Canada are St John's East, St John's South–Mount Pearl, Charlottetown, Dartmouth–Cole Harbour, Halifax, Moncton–Riverview–Dieppe, and Saint John. In addition, there are four mixed ridings with a substantial urban component, but also significant rural extent: Halifax West, Sackville–Eastern Shore, Sydney–Victoria, and Fredericton. The remaining 21 federal ridings in Atlantic Canada are geographically extensive and do not include large cities, so they would reasonably be categorized as mostly rural.

14 Dianne Brushett was the Liberal candidate in North Nova, the riding of long-time Conservative MP Bill Casey; Alexis MacDonald ran for the NDP, and Susan Green for the Liberals, against Conservative deputy leader (and former leader of the Progressive Conservative Party) Peter MacKay in Central Nova; Angela Vautour was the Conservative candidate in Beauséjour, running against Liberal deputy government whip, Dominic LeBlanc, and Mary Crane ran for the Conservatives in Malpeque against long-time Liberal MP and former solicitor general, Wayne Easter. In each case the incumbent won more than 50 per cent more votes than the second-place candidate.

15 The percentages listed indicate the proportion of women corresponding to each cell in the table. For example, 13 urban seats in the four provincial legislatures were won by the NDP: 5 by women and 8 by men. The proportion of women for this group of seats is therefore 38 per cent (5 of 13).

16 The preceding set of provincial elections in 1999 and 2000 had almost exactly the same result: 27 per cent of urban-centre ridings won by women, compared with 12 per cent of more rural ridings.

17 Personal communication at a public gathering in 2000.

18 Most voters in Atlantic Canada continue to support either the Liberal Party or the Conservative Party, in the same system of two-party competition that has structured elections from before Confederation. Any number of new parties – Social Credit, CCF, NDP, Reform, and Canadian Alliance – on the national stage has failed to make major inroads with the voters of Atlantic Canada. After the PC Party collapsed as a national party in the wake of its disastrous defeat in 1993, it retreated to its Atlantic bastion. New Brunswick has seen some, albeit short-lived, innovation in partisanship at the provincial level with the Acadian Party in the 1970s and the Confederation of Regions Party in the early 1990s. Both were absorbed into the dominant Liberal and Conservative parties, respectively. The 1997 general election seemed to promise a breakthrough for the NDP in the region when the NDP won 24 per cent of the popular vote, but it lost ground in the 2000 election as its share of the popular vote fell to 17 per cent (O'Neill and Erickson 2003). The NDP has been most successful in the urban core of Halifax, at the provincial level, where it appears to have secured a firm beachhead across several elections.

19 In a related finding in western Canada, Anthony Sayers found that election campaigns in selected rural districts of British Columbia were more 'substantial' because local media outlets focus exclusively on local candidates and local issues. Unlike the urban media, they do not feel obliged to cover national and international affairs. Local candidates can also afford to advertise more extensively in local media outlets whose costs are lower than national outlets; they also advertise more effectively because the distribution range of local media outlets is co-terminous with electoral boundaries (1999, 119–21).

2 An Interview Series in Atlantic Canada

1 Recruiting students in groups for the OTT program can be an overwhelming task for fieldworkers. One fieldworker explained that training to be a machinist or a pipefitter appeals to few women anywhere, and of these, few

were able to commit to spending such a long period at a college campus that was some distance from home. Most of the students in her current group were women who had not completed high school, had only ever worked in the local fish-processing plant, were married with children, and whose lives were in disarray. On the day when this fieldworker spoke to me, she was particularly discouraged because several recruits had withdrawn after learning that the local fish plant where their husbands worked was closing, as their families were planning to move away.

2 One example of interviewees contradicting my preconception relates to the role of sex and alcohol in politics. Alcohol has had a long and central place in Canadian politics. Until the mid-twentieth century, elections were raucously drunken events in which voters were 'treated' with a bottle in exchange for their support. Even as the heavy consumption of alcohol has been purged from the polling station (Stewart 1994, 64–72), rumours persist that it remains prevalent in the backrooms where party insiders gather to strategize. I suggested to participants that the heavy consumption of alcohol among men and women together is typically thought to create a sexually charged atmosphere, and may thereby act as a barrier to women's involvement at higher levels of politics. Interviewees overwhelmingly rejected this proposition. While some women spoke of the persistence of backroom drinking, very few thought that it was central to climbing the political ladder, and none reported any threat from a sexualized atmosphere.

3 An official from HRDC in Ottawa bristled at my suggestion that the WRDC was anything but an autonomous grassroots organization.

3 Leadership Characteristics of the Interviewees

1 *Caring Canadians, involved Canadians: Highlights from the 1997 national survey of giving, volunteering, and participating* (Statistics Canada catalogue no. 71–542–XPE, Aug. 1998).

2 Even if one includes the census respondents who reported the much more general 'other non-university education' along with university, the proportions in the districts studied are still well below 50 per cent.

3 The marital status of the other 38 interviewees divided into three nearly equal groups: 13 single, 14 divorced, and 11 widowed.

4 The numerical values were arbitrarily chosen in the simplest possible ascending scale. Other choices are possible; however, any reasonable choice leads to the same robust conclusions about the overall educational patterns.

5 One might imagine a pattern of decreasing education with age by looking at only the first four columns; however, that trend is very weak and, moreover,

inconsistent with the especially highly educated oldest age group in the fifth column.

6 No inference should be drawn about employment levels among rural women leaders from the responses to this question, which asked for the respondent's main occupation, regardless of current employment status, i.e., regardless of whether the respondent was employed, retired, unemployed, no longer looking for paid employment, and so on. Employment status is discussed later, in reference to a different question on the questionnaire.

7 This relationship was investigated using the ANOVA procedure to test for differences among groups of respondents sorted by employment status; the result of this calculation indicates that the probability of group differences this large arising by chance alone is only $p = .023$.

8 The ANOVA calculation (analogous to that described in the previous note) yields $p = .004$.

9 The ANOVA calculation yields $p = .012$.

10 The ANOVA calculation yields $p = .014$ for age-group differentiation on this question.

11 One of the 36 women who reported being a party member did not report which party.

12 Another ten women did not answer this question. A non-answer could mean either that the respondent did not feel close to any party or, alternatively, that she did not want to reveal her affiliation.

4 Images of Leadership

1 Unpublished in-person interview conducted by the author in 1994.

2 Acknowledgments are due to Amy Biggers for graphic alterations and to Josephine Vasiento for posing. Leonie Huddy and associates bear no responsibility for how the photos were used in this project, nor for the interpretation of results.

3 'Jane Politician' or 'John Politician' are used to refer to elected officials who appear in the transcript by their proper names.

4 If anything, there was probably a social desirability bias *against* choosing local figures, since the respondents were filling out the questionnaire for me and were aware that I would not recognize the names of most local figures.

5 Edith Archibald (1854–1936) used her high social position as wife of the president of the Bank of Nova Scotia to work for the cause of temperance as the president of the Woman's Christian Temperance Union, which, under her leadership advocated women's suffrage. See 'Foremothers in Equality:

Some Early Nova Scotia Suffragists' (N.S. Advisory Council on the Status of Women, Feb. 2003).

6 Although born in Quebec, Armine Gosling (1861–1942) moved to Newfoundland at age 21 to become a school principal. She was a gifted speaker and writer who worked against the unjust treatment of women and children, a cause that led her to a leading role in Newfoundland's suffrage movement. See Margot Duley, *Where once our mothers stood we stand: Women's suffrage in Newfoundland, 1890–1925* (Charlottetown: Gynergy, 1993).

7 Gladys Muriel Porter (1894–1967) was the first woman elected to the Nova Scotia Legislative Assembly, in 1960, and she held the seat until her death in 1967. The Progressive Conservative Party of Nova Scotia operates the 'Gladys Porter Fund' for female candidates. She lived her adult life in Kentville, which makes her an authentic rural woman leader. She was the first woman in the Maritimes to be elected as mayor, in 1946, when she was elected to that position in Kentville. Her father had been long-time mayor of Sydney, so she came from a political family. She was mayor of Kentville until she won the provincial seat for Kings North. She was a founding member and first president of the local chapter of the Business and Professional Women's Club. See *Canadian who's who*, vol. 9, *1961–63* (Toronto: Trans-Canada Press, 1963, 900); 'Mrs G.M. Porter, former Kentville mayor, MLA dies,' *Halifax Chronicle Herald*, 1 May 1967, 1–2; *Legislative Assembly of Nova Scotia 1758–1983: A biographical directory*, ed. Shirley Elliott (Halifax: Province of Nova Scotia, 1984, 177–8).

8 The Hon. Muriel McQueen Fergusson (1899–1997) was appointed to the Senate of Canada in 1953 as a Liberal; in 1972 she was appointed first female Speaker of Senate. She followed her father into law and was admitted to the New Brunswick Bar in 1925. When her husband died in 1942, she took over his law practice. She became the first director of the Family Allowance and later the Old Age Security programs in New Brunswick. She was the first woman elected to the Fredericton city council, and later the first woman deputy mayor of that city until her appointment to the Senate. She is now best known for the endowment fund named in her honour. See James Macgowan, 'Lives lived: Muriel McQueen Fergusson,' *Globe and Mail*, 5 May 1997, A16; Constance Mungall, 'Pattern-breakers of New Brunswick,' *Chatelaine* 50:7 (July 1977), 31, 51.

9 Lady Helena Squires (1879–1959) was the first woman elected to the Newfoundland House of Assembly (albeit in a by-election as the prime minister's wife), in 1930, when Newfoundland was still a separate dominion. Ironically, she had opposed the efforts of the Women's Suffrage League in the early 1920s during her husband's first term as prime minister. The fall of her hus-

band's Liberal government in 1932 was preceded by dramatic events, including a riot that trapped the couple in the House of Assembly. Lady Squires returned to public life in 1949, after Newfoundland joined Canada, when she was elected the first president of the Liberal Association of Newfoundland. See 'First lady elected to Parliament in Newfoundland,' *Newfoundland Quarterly* 30:1 (July 1930), 14–15; 'Squires, Helena,' *Encyclopedia of Newfoundland and Labrador* (St John's: Harry Cuff Publications, 1994).

5 The Slushy Intersection between Politics and Family

1 It can also be said that urban politicians have obligations that are not shared to the same extent by rural politicians, e.g., urban representatives tend to perform a great deal of work on behalf of relatives of constituents who wish to immigrate to Canada.

2 More precisely, it should be called the equivalent seat, given the changes to electoral boundaries and name of the riding that occurred over this lengthy period. The core of this riding was called Central Nova when represented by Elmer MacKay.

3 Lynn Verge was member of the Newfoundland House of Assembly (1979–1996); she became leader of the PC Party in 1995 and resigned after losing the 1996 election to the Liberal Party led by Brian Tobin.

4 Eleanor Norrie was an MLA for Truro-Bible Hill (1993–1997); she also held several cabinet portfolios in the Liberal Party government during that time. Before becoming an elected public official, she had been a restaurant owner and manager in the Truro area for more than 20 years. Her mother-in-law was Margaret Fawcett Norrie, appointed to the Senate of Canada in 1972, as a Liberal.

5 Recognition of the importance of gatekeepers also led to the 'sacrificial lamb' hypothesis, that is, that parties are more likely to nominate women as candidates for seats that they do not expect to win. In a quantitative analysis of women's candidacy from 1975 to 1994, Donley Studlar and Richard Matland found some evidence, albeit limited, supporting the sacrificial-lamb hypothesis in the 1970s. However, they found no evidence for this practice after the early 1980s (1996, 291), neither did Rejean Pelletier and Manon Tremblay in the case of Quebec, after taking political party into account (1992; see also Tremblay 1995). The hypothesis arose principally from the many women running as candidates for the NDP in ridings where the party was not competitive; and also from the fact that incumbents, most of whom are men, have an advantage. But when women run in open seats for a competitive party, they stand as fair a chance as men of being elected.

6 The introduction of new campaign finance legislation in 2003 now regulates nomination contests in national elections. This law requires all candidates running for a party's nomination to register with Elections Canada, and it requires candidates who spent more than $1,000 in their nomination bid to disclose contributions and expenditures. Spending on nomination campaigns is limited to 20 per cent of the maximum amount of spending allowed in the general election campaign. Just as in the election campaign itself, a nomination candidate may contribute up to $5,000 to her own candidacy, but corporations and trade unions are restricted to donating up to a total of $1,000 to any segment of the electoral process in a calendar year (Cross 2004, 166). Provincial nomination campaigns in the Atlantic Provinces are not governed by comparable regulations.

6 The Slushy Intersection between Politics and Occupation

1 While employment statistics about the not-for-profit sector are difficult to come by (due to the autonomous status of the relevant organizations), it seems safe to assume that it, too, employs a disproportionate number of women. In particular the organizations specifically directed at women commonly employ women to deliver services and often appoint women to the governing boards.
2 The executive director of a not-for-profit organization is often referred to as a 'public sector entrepreneur,' as they are responsible for cobbling together year-to-year funding that is never guaranteed.
3 These same considerations help to explain why this profession was particularly over-represented among the interviewees in this project (see Chapter 3).

7 The Slushy Intersection between Politics and the Local Economy

1 Toll-gating is the practice by which a governing party raises campaign funds by charging companies for access to public sector contracts. One notorious example was the RCMP investigation of the practice in Nova Scotia during the 1970s, which found that liquor companies gave a fixed percentage of sales to the governing Liberal Party in exchange for their products being sold in provincial government liquor stores. The typical fee was fifty cents a case of liquor (Simpson 1988, 183). The corporations involved were major national firms (Shenley and Jordan Wines) for whom such fees could be accommodated as a cost of doing business. In contrast, it is hard to see how a small business, operating at the margins of profitability and barely supporting a living wage for its owners, could afford to trade in partisan favours.

2 The original meaning of this word is a relic from feudal relations between landlords and tenant farmers; patrons were custodians of inherited family estates, who were responsible for the subsistence of their clients (the tenants). Some of this original meaning is incorporated in the contemporary use of the term 'clientelism' to describe politicians in analogous environments as patrons (Noel 1976).

3 Fred McMahon made just this point, claiming that labour shortages are unintended consequences of public policy (2000, 94–7).

4 Tom Blackwell, 'Liberals stand by candidate once jailed for defrauding EI,' *National Post*, 14 March 2003, A7. 'Payne's conviction a "plus": Grimes,' 10 October 2003, available at stjohns.cbc.ca/regional/servlet/View? filename=nf_payne_20031010, accessed 20 Jan. 2005. 'Newfoundland & Labrador Votes 2003,' 21 October 2003, available at www.cbc.ca/ nlvotes2003/riding/0310, accessed 20 Jan. 2005.

5 Kirkpatrick (1974) found that women politicians were more likely to be motivated by public service than by personal ambition or partisan rivalry.

6 'MacAulay in conflict controversy,' *CBC Online News*, 29 May 2002 Prince Edward Island News in Review, available at http://pei.cc.ca/newsinreview/ pei_macaulayconflict.html, accessed 20 Jan. 2005.

7 Norman Spector, 'Lawrence of ACOA,' *Globe and Mail*, 23 October 2002, A23.

8 This interviewee's comments are corroborated by Douglas House, who wrote that 'as a result of pressure from the community (people who needed work to qualify for UI [Employment Insurance] and thereby for basic income security for their families) and from government departments (officials who needed local agents for the make-work projects), RDAs in many instances found themselves operating mainly as the local administrators of short-term make-work programs' (1999, 181).

9 After the moratorium on the cod fishery in 1995, HRDC paid funds to individuals through the the Atlantic Groundfish Strategy (TAGS) Package which, in effect, bought people out of the industry. As fish harvesters and processors, some of the women in the discussion group would have qualified for the 'Package' as it came to be called. TAGS expired prior to 1999.

8 Structural Contours of Rural Women's Leadership in Atlantic Canada

1 Civic engagement may be studied under the rubric of social capital, a term which conceptualizes associational ties that foster trust and cooperation as a form of capital to be invested and thus produce wealth. The applied fields of development studies and public management refer to the matter of capacity

building and social cohesion in the context of communities acquiring the skills – in terms of individual personnel and collective cohesion – to plan goals for the future and administer resources in order to achieve that desired future. Voluntary associations cannot, of course, prevent ecological disasters or crises of globalization. Michael Walzer put a limited claim that associations may enable people to cope better with those crises and, hence, resist the deterioration of their communities thus: 'Dominated and deprived individuals are likely to be disorganized as well as impoverished, whereas poor people with strong families, churches, unions, political parties, and ethnic alliances are not likely to be dominated or deprived for long' (1995, 148).

2 One could debate the practical significance of this shift by citing continued public sector investment in large-scale industrial ventures in the automotive and aerospace industries in Ontario and Quebec. Entering into this general debate would take us beyond the scope of the present work. The important point here is that there was a meaningful shift in Atlantic Canada.

3 New information technologies and other components of the postindustrial service sector were seen to offer new opportunities for rural economies, for example, international call centres which can be located anywhere in the world. Tourism was considered to be another promising opportunity.

4 It seems natural that these criticisms might be countered from the left under the rubric of distributive justice, but the matter is strikingly under-theorized. Whereas the moral claims of refugees and immigrants attract much intellectual interest in terms of the concept of global citizenship, less attention is given to the internal displacement of Canadians brought about by the same global processes. One exception appeared in Glynis George's ethnographic account of the Women's Centre in Stephenville, Newfoundland (2000). George asserted a moral claim to settlement – a right to stay with one's extended family – which she applied to this isolated and deprived area of the North American periphery.

5 Siegel cited the example of a part-time mayor who partly owns one of three travel agencies in town to show how difficult it is to avoid conflict-of-interest situations. To prohibit the mayor's travel agency from doing work for the municipality would be too big a sacrifice for the travel agency, and the mayor would prefer to resign. Even were more strict regulations to be legislated in Canada, the basic problem would still remain that politicians can be tempted to make public policy decisions based on their personal financial interests (1993, 218–19).

6 In 2001, 19.5 per cent of individual income in Melfort, Saskatchewan, came from government transfers. This level is comparable with 17 per cent in St

George, NB, or 22 per cent in Shelburne, NS, and is far greater than the 7 per cent found in Fort St John, B.C. (Statistics Canada, Community Profiles).

7 The Liberal Women's Commission (LWC) is designed to provide an institutional structure for networking, mentoring, and helping women to move seamlessly between national and provincial levels; however, this project found little evidence for impact in rural Atlantic Canada. Even less so for the PC Party, which had fewer powerful women politicians at the centre. The new national Conservative Party of Canada does not have a separate women's organization, analogous to the LWC, that might serve as a mechanism for networking and mentoring; however, it could be said that the non-partisan bureaucracy has taken up the initiative, instead. In 2003–4, the Nova Scotia Advisory Council on the Status of Women undertook a series of political participation workshops across the province and inaugurated a women's campaign school for the entire Atlantic region, with special attention to rural participation. One suspects that the council's program is a convenient vehicle for the Conservative governments in the region to promote women's candidacy, while disavowing, in principle, any sort of affirmative action measures.

8 Similarly, Bourke and Luloff's study of rural Pennsylvania community leaders found that 'younger, college-educated women who were directors of local and county agencies, usually involving economic development, were recognized as leaders due to their position' (1997, 15).

9 This expectation would follow the example of U.S. state assemblies, which first saw significant increases in women elected in the less-professionalized, amateur assemblies of the small New England states during the 1970s, when the job held considerably less power and prestige (Thomas 1994, 144–6).

10 For example, Maurice Beaudin noted that 'when examined on a regional basis, the relative size of the public sector is greater in ... Halifax [where] the public sector contributes ... 33.5 percent of jobs and 41 percent of employment income' (1998, 47). Despite the heavy reliance of this major urban centre on the public sector, most of the expenditures involve relatively stable program spending. MPs and MLAs in Halifax ridings have little influence over the expenditures of the Department of National Defence, or the universities, or the Port Authority. The budgets of these institutions may go up or down, but usually only incrementally from year to year. Hence, the continued vitality of these pillars of the economy does not rest on the choice of elected representative, and the voters and riding associations know it.

11 Lublin and Brewer argued that the fact that urban electoral districts with higher levels of education and income tend to elect greater proportions of women to public office is not proof of more egalitarian attitudes in those dis-

tricts. Instead, they see it as proof of the lower desirability of the job in those high-income districts. Where private sector incomes are relatively high compared with the salaries attached to public office, standing for election carries a higher opportunity cost than in lower income districts (2003, 383–4).

12 The NDP's commitment to gender equity has demonstrably propelled women into public office in other regions of Canada, in elections in which it has won substantial numbers of seats. In the 1990s three provinces governed by the NDP stood out in this regard: British Columbia, under the leadership of Mike Harcourt and Glen Clark; Saskatchewan, under Roy Romanow; and Ontario, under Bob Rae. Each of these governments brought large increases in proportions of women elected. A dramatic example of the converse effect occurred in 1995, when Mike Harris's 'Common Sense Revolution' led the Ontario PC Party to victory over Bob Rae's NDP government – the proportion of women elected to Queen's Park fell back roughly to the pre-NDP level in that election.

References

Alasia, Alessandro. 1996. *Mapping the socio-economic diversity of rural Canada: A multivariate analysis.* Ottawa: Statistics Canada Research Paper.

Alberts, Sheldon. 2003. 'Is he the real MacKay?' *National Post,* 26 May, A6.

Arscott, Jane. 1997. 'Between the rock and a hard place: Women legislators in Newfoundland and Nova Scotia.' In *In the presence of women: Representation in Canadian governments.* Ed. Jane Arscott and Linda Trimble. Toronto: Harcourt Brace, 308–37.

Bashevkin, Sylvia. 1991. 'Women's participation in political parties.' In *Women in Canadian politics: Toward equity in representation* Ed. Kathy Megyery. Vol. 6 of the Research Studies of the Royal Commission on Electoral Reform and Party Financing. Ottawa and Toronto: RCERPF/Dundurn Press.

– 1985. *Toeing the lines: Women in party politics in English Canada.* Toronto: University of Toronto Press.

Beaudin, Maurice. 1998. *The economic region of Prince Edward Island.* Moncton: Canadian Institute for Research on Regional Development.

Bickerton, James. 1994. 'Atlantic Canada: Regime change in a dependent region.' In *Canadian Politics.* Ed. James Bickerton and Alain Gagnon. Peterborough, ON: Broadview, 426–49.

– 1990. *Politics of regional development in Nova Scotia.* Toronto: University of Toronto Press.

Blais, André, Elisabeth Gidengil, Agnieszka Dobrzynska, Neil Nevitte, and Richard Nadeau. 2003. 'Does the local candidate matter? Candidate effects in the Canadian election of 2000.' *Canadian Journal of Political Science* 36:3, 657–65.

Black, Naomi, and Gail Cuthbert Brandt. 1999. *Feminist politics on the farm: Rural Catholic women in southern Quebec and southwestern France.* Montreal: McGill-Queen's University Press.

Blake, Donald. 2001. *Electoral democracy in the provinces.* Montreal: Institute for Research on Public Policy.

Bollman, Ray D. ed. 2003. 'The gender balance of employment in rural and small town Canada.' *Rural and small town Canada analysis bulletin* 4:3. Statistics Canada, catalogue no. 21-006-XIE.

– 2001. 'Employment in rural and small town Canada: An update to 2000.' *Rural and small town Canada analysis bulletin* 3:4. Ottawa: Statistics Canada, catalogue no. 21–006–XIE.

– Ed. 2000. 'Factors associated with female employment in rural and small town Canada: An update to 2000.' *Rural and small town Canada analysis bulletin* 2:1. Ottawa: Statistics Canada, catalogue no. 21-006-XIE.

Bourke, Lisa, and A.E. Luloff. 1997. 'Women and leadership in rural areas.' *Women & Politics* 17: 1–23.

Brodie, Janine. 1977. 'The recruitment of Canadian women as provincial legislators, 1950–1975.' *Atlantis* 2: 6–17.

Brodie, Janine, with Celia Chandler. 1991. 'Women and the electoral process in Canada.' In *Women in Canadian politics: Toward equity in representation.* Ed. Kathy Megyery. Vol. 6 of the Research Studies of the Royal Commission on Electoral Reform and Party Financing. Ottawa and Toronto: RCERPF/ Dundurn Press.

Buckley, Sandra. 1994. 'A short history of the feminist movement in Japan.' In *Women of Japan and Korea.* Ed. Joyce Gelb and Marian Lief Palley. Philadelphia: Temple University Press.

Burns, Nancy, Kay Lehman Schlozman, and Sidney Verba. 2001. *The private roots of public action: Gender, equality, and political participation.* Cambridge, MA: Harvard University Press.

Burrell, Barbara. 1994. *A woman's place is in the house: Campaigning for Congress in the feminist era.* Ann Arbor: University of Michigan Press.

Burt, Sandra, and Elizabeth Lorenzin. 1997. 'Taking the women's movement to Queen's Park: Women's interests and the New Democratic Party government of Ontario.' In *In the presence of women: Representation in Canadian governments.* Ed. Jane Arscott and Linda Trimble. Toronto: Harcourt Brace, 202–27.

Carbert, Louise. 2002. 'Building social capital: Civic engagement in farm communities.' In *Political behaviour: Theory and practice in a Canadian context.* Ed. Joanna Everitt and Brenda O'Neill. Toronto: Oxford University Press, 297–314.

– 1995. *Agrarian feminism: The politics of Ontario farm women.* Toronto: University of Toronto Press.

Carbert, Louise, and Naomi Black. 2003. 'Building women's leadership in Atlantic Canada.' *Atlantis* 27:2, 72–8.

Carstairs, Sharon. 2000. 'Politics: Is it a woman's game?' In *Dropped Threads.* Ed. Carol Shields and Margaret Atwood. Toronto: Vintage Canada, 309–16.

Carty, Kenneth R., and Munroe Eagles. 2005. *Politics is local: National politics at the grassroots.* Don Mills, ON: Oxford University Press.

Clancy, Mary. 2003. 'Introductory remarks'. *Atlantis* 27:2, 79–81.

Coleman, Isobel. 2003. 'Women – A moderating influence on Islamic fundamentalism.' *Princeton Independent.* Feb., 11–12.

Conrad, Margaret. 2003. 'Addressing the democratic deficit: Women and political culture in Atlantic Canada.' *Atlantis* 27:2, 82–9.

Conrad, Margaret, and James K. Hiller. 2001. *Atlantic Canada: A region in the making.* Toronto: Oxford University Press.

Corporate Research Associates. 2002. *ACOA 2002 awareness and perception qualitative study.* Halifax: Corporate Research Associates.

Coxe, Donald. 2003. 'Buried treasures' *Maclean's* 116:43 (27 Oct.) 74.

Cross, William. 2004. *Political parties.* Vancouver: UBC Press.

– 2002. 'Grassroots participation in candidate nominations.' In *Citizen politics: Research and theory in Canadian political behaviour.* Ed. Joanna Everitt and Brenda O'Neill. Toronto: Oxford University Press.

Crossley, John. 1997. 'Picture this: Women politicians hold key posts in Prince Edward Island.' In *In the presence of women: Representation in Canadian governments.* Ed. Jane Arscott and Linda Trimble. Toronto: Harcourt Brace, 278–307.

Darcy, R., Susan Welch, and Janet Clark. 1994. *Women, elections, and representation.* 2nd ed. Lincoln: University of Nebraska Press.

Desserud, Don. 1997. 'Women in New Brunswick politics: Waiting for the third wave.' In *In the presence of women: Representation in Canadian governments.* Ed. Jane Arscott and Linda Trimble. Toronto: Harcourt Brace, 254–77.

Diochon, Monica. 2003. *Entrepreneurship and community economic development.* Montreal and Kingston: McGill-Queen's University Press.

Erickson, Lynda. 1998. 'Entry to the Commons: Parties, recruitment and the election of women in 1993.' In *Women and political representation in Canada.* Ed. Manon Tremblay and Caroline Andrew. Ottawa: University of Ottawa Press, 219–56.

Everitt, Joanna. 2003. 'Media in the Maritimes: Do female candidates face a bias?' *Atlantis* 27:2, 90–8.

Fern, Edward. 2001. *Advanced focus group research.* Thousand Oaks, CA: Sage.

Fort McMurray Historical Society. 1996. *The history of Fort McMurray.* Available at collections.ic.gc.ca/fortmc. Accessed 28 October 2005.

Galloway, Gloria. 2003. 'Martin calls for 52 percent women MPs: He won't call election without more female candidates, leader-to-be says.' *Globe and Mail,* 14 Nov., A5.

George, Glynis. 2000. *The Rock where we stand: An ethnography of women's activism in Newfoundland.* Toronto: University of Toronto Press.

Gidengil, Elisabeth, and Joanna Everitt. 2002. 'Damned if you do, damned if you don't: Television news coverage of female party leaders.' In *Political parties, representation, and electoral democracy in Canada.* Ed. William Cross. Toronto: Oxford University Press, 223–37.

Glaser, James. 1996. *Race, campaign politics, and the realignment in the south.* New Haven: Yale University Press.

Good, David. 2003. *The politics of public management: The HRDC audit of grants and contributions.* Toronto: University of Toronto Press.

Greenbaum, Thomas. 2000. *Moderating focus groups: A practical guide for group facilitation.* Thousand Oaks, CA: Sage.

Greenwood, John. 2005. 'Gateway to the east: Prince Rupert, BC struggles to remake itself in the image in which it was conceived – After years of decline, town on brink of rebirth through link to China.' *National Post,* 16 April FP1.

Gregg, Allan. 2004. 'How to save democracy.' *Walrus,* 26–9 Sept.

Groves, Sharon. 2001. 'Afghan women speak out.' *Feminist Studies* 27:3 753–9.

Halpern, Monda. 2001. *And on that farm he had a wife: Ontario farm women and feminism, 1900–1970.* Montreal: McGill-Queen's University Press.

House, Douglas. 1999. *Against the tide: Battling for economic renewal in Newfoundland and Labrador.* Toronto: University of Toronto Press.

Huddy, Leonie. 1998. 'The social nature of political identity: Feminist image and feminist identity.' Paper presented at the annual meeting of the American Political Science Association, Boston.

Inglehart, Ronald. 1997. *Modernization and postmodernization.* Princeton: Princeton University Press.

Jaremko, Gordon. 2005. 'Fort St John leads parade in B.C. energy boom.' *Edmonton Journal,* 11 Oct. 1.

Kanter, Rosabeth Moss. 1977. 'Some effects of proportions on group life: Skewed sex ratios and responses to token women.' *American Journal of Sociology* 82:5, 965–90.

Kechnie, Margaret. 2003. *Organizing rural women: The Federated Women's Institutes of Ontario, 1897–1919.* Montreal: McGill-Queen's University Press.

Kirkpatrick, Jeane. 1974. *Political woman.* New York: Basic Books.

Krueger, Richard, and Mary Anne Casey. 2000. *Focus groups: A practical guide for applied research,* 3rd Ed. Thousand Oaks, CA: Sage.

Lasch, Christopher. 1995. *The revolt of the elites and the betrayal of democracy.* New York: Norton.

Lublin, David, and Sarah Brewer. 2003. 'The continued dominance of traditional gender roles in southern elections.' *Social Science Quarterly* 84:2, 379–96.

MacManus, Susan, Charles Bullock, Frances Akins, Laura Jane Hoffman, and Adam Newmark. 1998. 'Winning in my own backyard: County government, school board positions steadily more attractive to women candidates.' In *Women in politics: Outsiders or insiders*, 3rd ed. Ed. Lois Lovel Duke. Upper Saddle River, NJ: Prentice-Hall.

Mancuso, Maureen, Michael Atkinson, André Blais, Ian Greene, and Neil Nevitte. 1998. *A question of ethics: Canadians speak Out.* Toronto: Oxford University Press.

Matland, Richard, and Donley Studlar. 1998. 'Gender and the electoral opportunity structure in the Canadian provinces.' *Political Research Quarterly* 5: 117–40.

McDonough, Alexa. 2003. 'Commentary.' *Atlantis* 27:2, 140–3.

McMahon, Fred. 2000. *Retreat from growth: Atlantic Canada and the negative-sum economy.* Halifax: Atlantic Institute for Market Studies.

Megyery, Kathy. Ed. 1991. *Women in Canadian politics: Toward equity in representation.* Vol. 6 of the Research Studies of the Royal Commission on Electoral Reform and Party Financing. Ottawa and Toronto: RCERPF/Dundurn Press.

Michels, Roberto. 1962 [1915]. *Political parties: A sociological study of the oligarchical tendencies of modern democracy.* Trans. Eden and Cedar Paul. Intro. S.M. Lipset. New York: Free Press.

Milne, William. 1996. *The McKenna miracle: Myth or reality?* Toronto: University of Toronto Centre for Public Management.

Moncrief, Gary, and Joel Thompson. 1991. 'Urban and rural ridings and women in provincial politics: A note on female MLAs.' *Canadian Journal of Political Science* 24: 831–7.

Morgan, David. 2002. 'Focus group interviewing.' In *Handbook of interview research.* Ed. Jaber Gubrium and James Holstein. Thousand Oaks, CA: Sage.

Morton, Suzanne. 2000. 'Gender, place, and region: Thoughts on the state of women in Atlantic Canadian history.' *Atlantis* 25:1, 119–28.

Neal, Rusty. 1998. *Brotherhood economics: Women and co-operatives in Nova Scotia.* Sydney: University College of Cape Breton Press.

Nikiforuk, Andrew. 2003. 'Northern greed.' *Canadian Business* 76:9, 46–52.

Niven, David. 1998. *The missing majority: The recruitment of women as state legislative candidates.* Westport. CT: Praeger.

Noel, S.J.N. 1976. 'Leadership and clientelism.' In *The provincial political systems: Comparative essays.* Ed. David Bellamy, John Pammett, and Donald Rowan. Toronto: Methuen, 197–213.

Norris, Pippa. 1997. *Passages to power: Legislative recruitment in advanced democracies.* New York: Cambridge University Press.

OECD. 2002. *Territorial Reviews, Canada.* Paris: OECD.

O'Neill, Brenda, and Lynda Erickson. 2003. 'Evaluating traditionalism in the Atlantic provinces: Voting, public opinion and the electoral project?' *Atlantis* 27:2, 113–22.

Pelletier, Rejean, and Manon Tremblay. 1992. 'Les femmes sont-elles candidates dans des circonscriptions perdues d'avance? De l'examen d'une croyance.' *Revue canadienne de science politique* 25: 249–67.

Pharr, Susan. 1981. *Political women in Japan.* Berkeley: University of California Press.

Phillips, Anne. 1995. *The politics of presence.* Oxford: Clarendon.

Rayside, David. 1991. *A small town in modern times.* Montreal and Kingston: McGill-Queen's University Press.

Ross, Ian. 2005. 'Diamonds drive Wawa boom.' *Northern Ontario Business* 25:8, 11.

Royal Commission on Electoral Reform and Party Financing. 1991. *Reforming electoral democracy.* Vol. 1 of the Research Studies of the Royal Commission on Electoral Reform and Party Financing. Ottawa and Toronto: RCERPF/Dundurn Press.

Savoie, Donald. 2000. *Community economic development in Atlantic Canada: False hope or panacea?* Moncton: Canadian Institute for Research on Regional Development.

– 1997. *Rethinking Canada's regional development policy: An Atlantic perspective.* Moncton: Canadian Institute for Research on Regional Development.

Sayers, Anthony. 1999. *Parties, candidates, and constituency campaigns in Canadian elections.* Vancouver: UBC Press.

Siegel, David. 1993. 'Small-town Canada' In *Corruption, character, and conduct: Essays on Canadian government ethics.* Ed. John Langford and Allan Tupper. Toronto: Oxford University Press, 217–34.

Simpson, Jeffrey. 1988. *Spoils of power: The politics of patronage.* Toronto: Collins.

Statistics Canada. 1996. *Federal Electoral District Profile.* Available at http://www/2.statcan.ca/fedprofil/Eng/FedSelect_E.cfm.

Stewart, David. 2002. 'Political realignment in Atlantic Canada?' In *Regionalism and party politics in Canada.* Ed. Lisa Young and Keith Archer. Toronto: Oxford University Press, 171–87.

Stewart, David, and Prem Shamdasani. 1990. *Focus groups: Theory and practice,* vol. 20. Newbury Park, CA: Sage.

Stewart, Ian. 1994a. 'Despoiling the public sector? The case of Nova Scotia.' In *Corruption, character, and conduct: Essays on Canadian government ethics.* Ed. John Langford and Allan Tupper. Toronto: Oxford University Press, 90–112.

Stewart, Ian. 1994b. *Roasting chestnuts: The mythology of Maritime political culture* Vancouver: University of British Columbia Press.

Studlar, Donley, and Richard Matland. 1996. 'The dynamics of women's representation in the Canadian provinces, 1975–1994.' *Canadian Journal of Political Science* 29, 269–94.

Sutherland, Sharon. 2001. 'Biggest scandal in Canadian history': HRDC audit starts probity war.' *Working Paper* 23. Kingston: Queen's University School of Policy Studies.

Templeton, Jane Farley. 1994. *The focus group: A strategic guide to organizing, conducting and analyzing the focus group interview.* Toronto: McGraw-Hill.

Thomas, Sue. 1994. 'Women in state legislatures.' In *The year of the woman: Myths and realities.* Ed. Elizabeth Adell Cook, Sue Thomas, and Clyde Wilcox. Boulder, CO: Westview Press.

Tremblay, Manon. 2002. 'L'élection fédérale de 2000: Qu'est-il donc arrivé aux candidates?' *Politique et Sociétés* 21, 89–109.

– 1998. 'Do female MPs substantively represent women? A study of legislative behavior in Canada's 35th Parliament.' *Canadian Journal of Political Science* 31:3, 435–65.

– 1995. 'Les femmes, des candidates moins performantes que les hommes? Une analyse des votes obtenus par les candidates et candidats du Québec à une élection fédérale canadienne, 1945–1993.' *Revue internationale d'études canadiennes* 11, 59–81.

Tremblay, Manon and Rejean Pelletier. 2001. 'More women constituency party presidents: A strategy for increasing the number of women candidates in Canada?' *Party Politics* 7:157–90.

Trimble, Linda. 1997. 'Feminist politics in the Alberta legislature.' In *In the presence of women: Representation in Canadian governments.* Ed. Jane Arscott and Linda Trimble. Toronto: Harcourt Brace, 128–53.

Trimble, Linda, and Jane Arscott. 2003. *Still counting: Women in politics across Canada.* Peterborough, ON: Broadview Press.

Verba, Sidney, Kay Lehman Schlozman, and Henry Brady. 1995. *Voice and equality: Civic voluntarism in American politics.* Cambridge, MA: Harvard University Press.

Vickers, Jill. 1997. 'Toward a feminist understanding of representation.' In *In the presence of women: Representation in Canadian governments.* Ed. Jane Arscott and Linda Trimble. Toronto: Harcourt Brace, 20–46.

Walzer, Michael. 1995. 'The idea of civil society.' In *Braving the new world.* Ed. Thomas Bateman, Manuel Mertin, and David Thomas. Toronto: Nelson, 142–53.

Young, Iris Marion. 1990. *Justice and the politics of difference.* Princeton: Princeton University Press.

Young, Lisa. 2003. 'Can feminists transform party politcs? The Canadian experience.' In *Women and electoral politics in Canada.* Ed. Manon Tremblay and Linda Trimble. Toronto: Oxford University Press, 76–91.

– 1991. 'Legislative turnover in the election of women to the Canadian House of Commons.' In *Women in Canadian politics: Toward equity in representation.* Ed.

by Kathy Megyery. Vol. 6 of the Research Studies of the Royal Commission on Electoral Reform and Party Financing. Ottawa and Toronto: RCERPF/Dundurn Press.

Young, Lisa, and Elaine Campbell. 2001. 'Women and political representation.' In *Political parties in Canada*, 8th ed. Ed. H. Thorburn and A. Whitehorn. Toronto: Prentice-Hall, 61–74.

Young, Lisa, and William Cross. 2003. 'Women's involvement in Canadian party politics.' In *Women and electoral politics in Canada*. Ed. Manon Tremblay and Linda Trimble. Toronto: Oxford University Press, 92–109.

Young, R.A. 1986. 'Teaching and research in Maritimes politics: Old stereotypes and new directions.' *Journal of Canadian Studies* 21:2, 133–55.

Index